The Christian's Secret of a Happy Life

The Christian's Secret of a Happy Life

Hannah Whitall Smith

BARBOUR
PUBLISHING

© 2010 by Barbour Publishing, Inc.

ISBN 978-1-60260-855-9

All scripture quotations are taken from the King James Version of the Bible.

Cover image © Susan Fox/Trevillion Images

Published by Barbour Publishing, Inc., P.O. Box 719, Uhrichsville, Ohio 44683, www.barbourbooks.com.

Our mission is to publish and distribute inspirational products offering exceptional value and biblical encouragement to the masses.

ecpa Member of the Evangelical Christian Publishers Association

Printed in the United States of America.

PART I

The Life

CHAPTER 1

Is It Scriptural?

No thoughtful person can question the fact that, for the most part, the Christian life, as it is generally lived, is not entirely a happy life. A keen observer once said, "You Christians seem to have a religion that makes you miserable. You are like a man with a headache. He does not want to get rid of his head, but it hurts him to keep it. You cannot expect outsiders to seek very earnestly for anything so uncomfortable." For the first time I saw that Christianity ought to make its possessors, not miserable, but happy. I asked the Lord to show me the secret of a happy Christian life. I shall share this secret.

In moments of illumination, God's children feel that a life of rest and victory is their birthright.

Remember the shout of triumph your souls gave when you first met the Lord Jesus and glimpsed His mighty saving power? How easy it seemed to be more than conquerors through Him who loved you! Under the leadership of a captain who had never been foiled in battle, how could you dream of defeat!

And yet, to many of you, how different your real experience has been! Your victories have been few and fleeting, your defeats many and disastrous. Christ is believed in, talked about, and served, but He is not known as the soul's actual and very life, abiding there forever and revealing Himself there continually in His beauty. You have found Jesus as your Savior from the penalty of sin, but you have not found Him as your Savior from sin's power. You have carefully studied the holy scriptures and have gathered much precious truth from them, which you hoped would feed and nourish your spiritual life. But in spite of it all, your souls are starving and dying within you, and you cry out in secret, again and again, for that bread and water of life that you see promised in the scriptures to all believers.

Your early visions of triumph have seemed to grow dimmer and dimmer, and you have been forced to settle down to the conviction that the best you can expect from your religion is a life of alternate failure and victory, one hour sinning and the next repenting, and then beginning again, only to fail again, and again to repent.

But *is* this all? Had the Lord Jesus only this in His mind when He laid down His precious life to deliver you from your difficult and cruel bondage to sin? Was there a hidden reserve in each promise that was meant to deprive it of its complete fulfillment? Can we dream that the Savior, who was wounded for our transgressions and bruised for our iniquities, could possibly see of the travail of His soul and be satisfied in such Christian lives as fill the Church today? The Bible tells us that "for this purpose the Son of God was manifested, that he might destroy the works of the devil"; and can we imagine for a moment that this is beyond His power and that He finds Himself unable to accomplish the thing He came to earth to do?

In the very beginning, then, settle down on this one thing, that Jesus came to save you, now, in this life, from the power and dominion of sin and to make you more than conquerors through His power. If you doubt this, search your Bible, and collect together every announcement or declaration concerning the purposes and object of His death on the cross. His work is to deliver us from our sins, from our bondage, from our defilement; and not a hint is given anywhere that this deliverance was limited and partial, one with which Christians so continually try to be satisfied.

When the angel of the Lord appeared unto Joseph in a dream and announced the coming birth of the Savior, he said, "And thou shalt call his name JESUS: for he shall save his people from their sins."

When Zacharias was "filled with the Holy Ghost" at the birth of his son, and "prophesied," he declared that God had visited His people in order to fulfill the promise and the oath He had made them, "that we being delivered out of the hand of our enemies might serve him without fear, in holiness and righteousness before him, all the days of our life."

When Peter was preaching in the porch of the temple to the wondering Jews, he said, "Unto you first God, having raised up his Son Jesus, sent him to bless you, in turning away every one of you from his iniquities."

When Paul told the Ephesian church the wondrous truth, that Christ had so loved them as to give Himself for them, he went on to declare that His purpose in doing this was "that he might sanctify and cleanse it with the washing of water by the word, that he might present it to himself a glorious church, not having spot, or wrinkle, or any such thing; but that it should be holy and without blemish."

When Paul was seeking to instruct Titus, his own son after the common faith, concerning the grace of God, he declared that the object of that grace was to teach us "that, denying ungodliness and worldly lusts, we should live soberly, righteously, and godly, in this present world." He then added the reason—that Christ "gave himself for us, that he might redeem us from all iniquity, and purify unto himself a peculiar people, zealous of good works."

When Peter encouraged the Christians, to whom he was writing, to walk holy and Christlike, he tells them that "even hereunto were ye called: because Christ also suffered for us, leaving us an example, that ye should follow his steps: who did not sin, neither was guile found in his mouth." He added, "Who his own self bare our sins in his own body on the tree, that we, being dead to sins, should live unto righteousness: by whose stripes ye were healed."

In Ephesians when Paul contrasted the walk suitable for a Christian with the walk of an unbeliever, he set before them the truth in Jesus as being this: "That ye put off concerning the former conversation the old man, which is corrupt according to the deceitful lusts; and be renewed in the spirit of your mind; and that ye put on the new man, which after God is created in righteousness and true holiness."

In Romans 6, Paul brought up the fact of our judicial death and resurrection with Christ as an unanswerable argument for our practical deliverance from sin. For a child of God to continue sinning is utterly foreign to the whole spirit and aim of the salvation of Jesus. He says, "God forbid. How shall we, that are dead to sin, live any longer therein? Know ye not, that so many of us as were baptized into Jesus Christ were baptized into his death? Therefore we are buried with him by baptism into death: that like as Christ was raised up from the dead by the glory of the Father, even so we also should walk in newness of life," and adds, "Knowing this, that our old man is crucified with him, that the body of sin might be destroyed, that henceforth we should not serve sin."

Sometimes we overlook the fact that there are far more references made of a present salvation from sin than of a future salvation in a heaven beyond.

Can we for a moment suppose that the holy God, who hates sin in the sinner, is willing to tolerate it in the Christian, and that He has even arranged the plan of salvation in such a way as to make it impossible for those who are saved from the guilt of sin to find deliverance from its power?

Dr. Chalmers says, "Sin is that scandal which must be rooted out from the great spiritual household over which the Divinity rejoices. Now that the penalty is taken off, do you think it is possible that the unchangeable God has so given up His antipathy to sin that man, ruined and redeemed, may now indulge in sin, which under the old order destroyed him? Does not the God who loved righteousness and hated iniquity six thousand years ago bear the same love to righteousness and hatred to iniquity still? The cross of Christ, by the same mighty and decisive stroke that moved the curse of sin away from us, also surely moves away the power and the love of it from over us."

The redemption accomplished for us by our Lord Jesus Christ on the cross at Calvary is a redemption from the power of sin as well as from its guilt. He *is* able to save to the uttermost all who come unto God by Him.

A quaint old Quaker divine of the seventeenth century says: "There is nothing so contrary to God as sin, and God will not suffer sin always to rule His masterpiece, man. When we consider God's inexhaustible power for destroying that which is contrary to Him, who can believe that the devil must always stand and prevail?

"It is inconsistent and disagreeable with the true faith for people to be Christians and yet to believe that Christ, the eternal Son of God, to whom all power in heaven and earth is given, will allow sin and the devil to have dominion over them.

"If you say sin is deeply rooted in man, I say so, too. But Christ Jesus has received power to destroy the devil and his works and to recover and redeem man into righteousness and holiness. Or else it is false that 'He is able to save to the uttermost all that come unto God by Him.' We must throw away the Bible if we say that it is impossible for God to deliver man out of sin.

"So, then, I do expect the benefit of my redemption and that I shall go out of my captivity. But still they say you must abide in sin as long as you live. What! Must we never be delivered? Must this crooked heart and perverse will always remain? Must I be a believer and yet have no faith that reaches to sanctification and holy living? Is there no mastery to be had, no getting victory over sin? Must it prevail over me as long as I live? What sort of a redeemer is this, or what benefit of my redemption do I have in this life?"

This isn't a new doctrine in the Church; however, much of it may have been lost sight of by the present generation of believers. It is the same old story that has filled the daily lives of many saints of God with songs of triumph throughout all ages; and it is now being sounded forth again to the unspeakable joy of weary and burdened souls.

Do not reject it until you have prayerfully searched the scriptures to see whether these things be indeed so. Ask God to open the eyes of your understanding by His Spirit that you may know "what is the exceeding greatness of his power to us-ward who believe, according to the working of his mighty power, which he wrought in Christ, when he raised him from the dead, and set him at his own right hand in the heavenly places." And when you have begun to have some faint glimpses of this power, learn to look away utterly from your own weakness, and, putting your case into His hands, trust Him to deliver you.

CHAPTER 2

God's Side and Man's Side

There are two very decided and distinct sides to this subject, and like all other subjects, it cannot be fully understood unless both of these sides are kept constantly in view. I refer of course to God's side and man's side; or, in other words, to God's part in the work of sanctification and man's part. These are very distinct and even contrasting, but they are not really contradictory, although to a casual observer they may appear so.

Suppose two friends go to see some celebrated building and return home to describe it. One has seen only the north side and the other only the south.

The first says, "The building was built in such a manner, and has such and such stories and ornaments."

"Oh no," says the other, interrupting him, "you are altogether mistaken. I saw the building, and it was built in quite a different manner, and its ornaments and stories were so and so."

A lively dispute might follow upon the truth of the respective descriptions until the two friends should discover that they had been describing different *sides* of the building, and then all would be reconciled at once.

I believe there are two distinct sides in this matter. But only looking at one without seeing the other is certain to create wrong impressions and views of the truth. In brief, man's part is to trust, and God's part is to work. There is certain *work* to accomplish. We are delivered from the power of sin and are made perfect in every good work to do the will of God. This real labor is worked in us and upon us. Besetting sins are conquered, evil habits are overcome, wrong dispositions and feelings are rooted out, and holy tempers and emotions are birthed. A positive transformation takes place. So at least the Bible teaches.

Most of us tried to do it for ourselves at first, and have grievously failed. Then we discover that we are unable to do it. But the Lord Jesus Christ has come on purpose to do it, and He will do it for all who put themselves wholly into His hands and trust Him without reserve.

Plainly the believer can do nothing but trust, while the Lord, in whom he trusts, actually does the work entrusted to Him. *Trusting* and *doing* are certainly contrasted things, often indeed contradictory, but are they contradictory in this case? Obviously not, because it is two different parties that are concerned. The preacher, who is speaking on man's part in the matter, cannot speak of anything but surrender and trust, because this is positively all the man can do. Such preachers are constantly criticized as though, in saying this, they had meant to imply there *was* no other part. The cry goes out that this doctrine of faith does away with all realities, that souls are just told to trust, and that they sit down from now on in a sort of religious easy chair, dreaming away a life, fruitless of any actual result. This misapprehension arises, of course, from the fact that either the preacher has neglected to state, or the hearer has failed to hear, the other side of the matter, which is, that when we trust, the Lord works, and that a great deal is done, not by us, but by Him. Actual results are reached by our trusting, because our Lord undertakes the thing entrusted to Him and accomplishes it. *We* do not do anything, but *He* does it. And it is all the more effectually done because of this. As soon as this is clearly seen, the difficulty as to the preaching of faith disappears entirely.

On the other hand, the preacher who dwells on God's part in the matter is criticized on a totally different ground. He does not speak of trust, for the Lord's part is not to trust but to work. The Lord's part is to *do* the thing entrusted to Him. He brings to bear upon us all the refining and purifying resources of His wisdom and His love, causing us to grow in grace and conforming us, day by day and hour by hour, to the image of Christ. Sanctification is both a step of faith and a process of works. It is a step of surrender and trust on our part, and it is a process of development on God's part. By a step of faith, we put ourselves into the hands of the divine Potter. By a gradual process, He makes us into a vessel unto His own honor. Suppose I were to describe to a person, who was entirely ignorant of the subject, the way in which a lump of clay is made into a beautiful vessel. I tell him first the part of the clay in the matter. All I can say about this is that the clay is put into the potter's hands and then lies passive there, submitting itself to all the turnings and overturnings of the potter's hands upon it. The potter takes the clay thus abandoned to his working and begins to mold and fashion it according to his own will. He kneads and works it; he tears it apart and presses it together again; he wets it and then suffers it to dry. Sometimes he works at it for hours together; sometimes he lays it aside for days and does not touch it. And then, when by all these processes he has made it perfectly pliable in his hands, he proceeds to make it up into the vessel he has proposed. He turns it upon the wheel, planes it, and smoothes it, and dries it in the sun, bakes it in the oven, and finally turns it out of his workshop, a vessel to his honor and fit for his use.

This is the clay's part in the matter. I now speak of the potter's part. These two are necessarily contrasted, but not in the least contradictory. The clay is not expected to do the potter's work, but only to yield itself up to his working.

Nothing, it seems to me, could be clearer than the perfect harmony between these two *apparently* contradictory sorts of teaching.

What *can* be said about man's part in this great work but that he must continually surrender himself and continually trust? When we come to God's side of the question, what is there that may not be said as to the many and wonderful ways in which He accomplishes the work entrusted to Him? It is here that the growing comes in. The lump of clay could never grow into a beautiful vessel if it stayed in the clay pit for thousands of years. But when it is put into the hands of a skillful potter, it grows rapidly, under his fashioning, into the vessel he intends it to be. And in the same way the soul abandoned to the working of the heavenly Potter is made into a vessel unto honor, sanctified, and meet for the Master's use.

Having, then, taken the step of faith by which you have put yourself wholly and absolutely into His hands, expect Him to begin to work. His way of accomplishing that which you have entrusted to Him may be different from your way, but He knows, and you must be satisfied.

I knew a lady who had entered into this life of faith with a great outpouring of the Spirit and a wonderful flood of light and joy. She supposed, of course, this was a preparation for some great service and expected to be put forth immediately into the Lord's harvest field. Instead of this, almost at once her own husband lost all his money, and she was shut up in her own house to attend to all sorts of domestic duties with no time or strength left for any gospel work at all. She accepted the discipline and yielded herself up as heartily to sweep and dust and bake and sew, as she would have done to teach, or pray, or write for the Lord. And the result was that, through this very training, He made her into a vessel "meet for the Master's use, and prepared unto every good work."

Another lady, who had entered this life of faith under similar circumstances of wondrous blessing and who also expected to be sent out to do some great work, was shut up with two peevish invalid children to nurse and humor and amuse all day long. Unlike the first one, this lady did not accept the training, but chafed and fretted, and finally rebelled, lost all her blessing, and went back into a state of sad coldness and misery. She had understood her part of trusting to begin with, but, not understanding the divine process of accomplishing that for which she had trusted, she took herself out of the hands of the heavenly Potter, and the vessel was marred on the wheel.

The maturity of a Christian experience cannot be reached in a moment but is the result of the work of God's Holy Spirit, who, by His energizing and transforming power, causes us to grow up into Christ in all things. And we cannot hope to reach this maturity in any other way than by yielding ourselves up, utterly and willingly, to His mighty working.

All that we claim, then, in this life of sanctification is that by an act of faith we put ourselves into the hands of the Lord, for Him to work in us all the good pleasure of His will, and then, by a continuous exercise of faith, keep ourselves there. When we do it, and while we do it, we are, in the scripture sense, truly pleasing God, although it may require years of training and discipline to mature us into a vessel that shall be in all respects to His honor and fitted to every good work.

Our part is the trusting; it is His to accomplish the results. And when we do our part, He never fails to do His, for no one ever trusted in the Lord and was destroyed. Do not be afraid, then, that if you trust or tell others to trust, the matter will end there. Trust is the beginning and the continuing foundation.

And this explains that apparent paradox that puzzles so many. They say, "In one breath you tell us to do nothing but trust, and in the next you tell us to do impossible things."

They are to reconciled, just as we reconcile the statements concerning a saw in a carpenter's shop, when we say, at one moment, that the saw has sawn asunder a log, and the next moment declare that the carpenter has done it. The saw is the instrument used; the power that uses it is the carpenter's.

In the divine order, God's working depends upon our cooperation. Of our Lord it was declared that at a certain place He could do there no mighty work because of their unbelief. It was not that He would not, but He could not. Just as the potter, however skillful, cannot make a beautiful vessel out of a lump of clay that is never put into his hands, so neither can God make out of me a vessel unto His honor unless I put myself into His hands. In this book, I shall of course dwell mostly upon man's side, as I am writing for human beings, in the hope of making it plain how we are to fulfill our part of this great work. But I wish it to be distinctly understood all through, that unless I believed with all my heart in God's effectual working on His side, not one word of this book would ever have been written.

CHAPTER 3
The Life Defined

The experience sometimes called the "higher Christian life" is the only true Christian life and is best described in the words "the life hid with Christ in God." The scriptures do set before the believer in the Lord Jesus a life of abiding rest and of continual victory, which is very far beyond the ordinary run of Christian experience. In the Bible we have presented to us a Savior able to save us from the power of our sins as really as He saves us from their guilt.

The chief characteristics of a life hid with Christ are an entire surrender to the Lord and a perfect trust in Him, resulting in victory over sin and inward rest of soul. It differs from the lower range of Christian experience in that it causes us to let the Lord carry our burdens and manage our affairs for us instead of trying to do it ourselves.

Most Christians are like a man who was toiling along the road, bending under a heavy burden, when a wagon overtook him, and the driver kindly offered to help him on his journey. He joyfully accepted the offer but, when seated in the wagon, continued to bend beneath his burden, which he still kept on his shoulders.

"Why do you not lay down your burden?" asked the kindhearted driver.

"Oh!" replied the man, "I feel that it is almost too much to ask you to carry me, and I could not think of letting you carry my burden, too."

And so Christians who have given themselves into the care and keeping of the Lord Jesus still continue to bend beneath the weight of their burdens and often go weary and heavy laden throughout the whole length of their journey.

When I speak of burdens, I mean everything that troubles us, whether spiritual or temporal.

First of all, the greatest burden we have to carry in life is self, and the most difficult thing we have to manage is self. Our own daily living, our frames and feelings, our special weaknesses and temptations, our peculiar temperaments, our inward affairs of every kind—these are the things that perplex and worry us more than anything else and that bring us most frequently into bondage and darkness. You must hand yourself, with your temptations, your temperament, your frames and feelings, and all your inward and outward experiences, over into the care and keeping of your God and leave it all there.

He made you, and therefore He understands you and knows how to manage you. You must trust Him to do it. Say to Him, "Here, Lord, I abandon myself to You. I have tried in every way I could think of to manage myself and to make myself what I know I ought to be, but I have always failed. Now I give it up to You. Take entire possession of me. Work in me all the good pleasure of Your will. Mold and fashion me into such a vessel as seems good to You. I leave myself in Your hands, and I believe You will, according to Your promise, make me into a vessel unto Your own honor, 'sanctified, and meet for the Master's use, and prepared unto every good work.' " And here you must rest, trusting yourself to Him, continually and absolutely.

Next, lay off every other burden—your health, your reputation, your Christian work, your houses, your children, your business, your servants—everything, in short, that concerns you, whether inward or outward.

It is generally much less difficult for us to commit the keeping of our future to the Lord than it is to commit our present. We know we are helpless as regards the future, but we feel as if the present was in our own hands and must be carried on

our own shoulders; and most of us have an unconfessed idea that it is a great deal to ask the Lord to
carry ourselves, and that we cannot think of asking Him to carry our burdens, too.

I knew a Christian lady who had a very heavy
temporal burden. It took away her sleep and
her appetite, and there was danger of her health
breaking down under it. One day, when it seemed
specially heavy, she noticed lying on the table near
her a little tract called *Hannah's Faith*. Attracted
by the title, she picked it up and began to read it,
little knowing, however, that it was to create a rev-
olution in her whole experience. The story was of
a poor woman who had been carried triumphantly
through a life of unusual sorrow.

She was giving the history of her life to a kind
visitor on one occasion, and at the close the visitor
said feelingly, "Oh, Hannah, I do not see how you
could bear so much sorrow!"

"I did not bear it," was the quick reply; "the
Lord bore it for me."

"Yes," said the visitor, "that is the right way.
We must take our troubles to the Lord."

"Yes," replied Hannah, "but we must do more
than that: *leave* them there. Most people," she
continued, "take their burdens to Him, but they
bring them away with them again and are just as
worried and unhappy as ever. But I take mine, and
I leave them with Him and come away and forget
them. If the worry comes back, I take it to Him

again; and I do this over and over until at last I just forget I have any worries and am at perfect rest."

It was a very simple secret she found out: It was possible to obey God's commandment contained in those words, "Be careful for nothing; but in every thing by prayer and supplication with thanksgiving let your requests be made known unto God"; and that in obeying it, the result would inevitably be, according to the promise, that the "peace of God, which passeth all understanding, shall keep your hearts and minds through Christ Jesus."

The soul who has discovered this secret of simple faith has found the key that will unlock the whole treasure-house of God.

Some child of God who is hungering for just such a life as I have been describing is reading this book. You long unspeakably to get rid of your weary burdens. You would be delighted to hand over the management of your unmanageable self into the hands of one who is able to manage you. Do you recollect the delicious sense of rest with which you have sometimes gone to bed at night after a day of great exertion and weariness? How delightful was the sensation of relaxing every muscle and letting your body go in a perfect abandonment of ease and comfort! You no longer had to hold up an aching head or a weary back. You trusted yourself to the bed in absolute confidence, and it held you up, without effort or strain or even thought on your part. You rested!

Suppose you had doubted the strength or the stability of your bed and had dreaded each moment to find it giving way beneath you and landing you on the floor. Could you have rested then? Would not every muscle have been strained in a fruitless effort to hold yourself up, and would not the weariness have been greater than if you had not gone to bed at all?

Let this analogy teach you what it means to rest in the Lord. Let your souls lie down upon the couch of His sweet will, as your bodies lie down in their beds at night. Relax every strain, and lay off every burden. Let yourself go in a perfect abandonment of ease and comfort, sure that, since He holds you up, you are perfectly safe. Your part is simply to rest. His part is to sustain you, and He cannot fail.

Take another analogy, which our Lord Himself has abundantly sanctioned—that of the child-life. For "Jesus called a little child unto him, and set him in the midst of them, and said, . . . Except ye be converted and become as little children, ye shall not enter into the kingdom of heaven."

What are the characteristics of a little child, and how does he live? He lives by faith, and his chief characteristic is freedom from care. His life is one long trust from year's end to year's end. He trusts his parents, he trusts his caretakers, he trusts his teachers. He even trusts people sometimes who are utterly unworthy of trust, out of the abounding trustfulness of his nature. The child provides nothing for himself, and yet everything is provided. He lives in the present moment and receives his life unquestioningly, as it comes to him day by day from his father's hand.

I was visiting once in a wealthy home where there was a little adopted child upon whom was lavished all the love and tenderness and care that human hearts could bestow or human means procure. And as I watched that child running in and out day by day, free and lighthearted with the happy carelessness of childhood, I thought what a picture it was of our wonderful position as children in the house of our heavenly Father. How much more must the great, loving heart of our God and Father be grieved and wounded at seeing His children taking so much anxious care and thought! Who is the best cared for in every household? Is it not the little children? And does not the least of all, the helpless baby, receive the largest share? We all know that the baby toils not, neither does he spin; and yet he is fed and clothed and loved and rejoiced in more tenderly than the hardest worker of them all.

This life of faith consists in just this—being a child in the Father's house.

Let the ways of childish confidence and freedom from care, which so please you and win your hearts in your own little ones, teach you what should be your ways with God. Leaving yourselves in His hands, learn to be literally "careful for nothing," and you shall find it a fact that the peace of God, which passes all understanding, shall keep (as with a garrison) your hearts and minds through Christ Jesus.

It is no speculative theory. Neither is it a dream of romance. There *is* such a thing as having one's soul kept in perfect peace, now and here in this life; and childlike trust in God is the key to its attainment.

CHAPTER 4

How to Enter In

This blessed life must not be looked upon in any sense as an attainment but as an obtainment. We cannot earn it; we cannot climb up to it; we cannot win it; we can do nothing but ask for it and receive it. It is the gift of God in Christ Jesus. And where a thing is a gift, the only course left for the receiver is to take it and thank the giver. In order, therefore, to enter into a practical experience of this interior life, the soul must be in a receptive attitude, fully recognizing the fact that it is God's gift in Christ Jesus, and that we cannot gain it by any efforts or works of our own. He can bestow it only upon the fully consecrated soul, and it is received by faith.

I was once trying to explain to a physician who had charge of a large hospital the necessity and meaning of consecration, but he seemed unable to understand. At last I said to him, "Suppose, in going your rounds among your patients, you should meet a man who entreated you earnestly to take his case under your special care in order to cure him. At the same time he refused to tell you all his symptoms or to take all your prescribed remedies. Suppose he should say to you, 'I am quite willing to follow your directions as to certain things, because they commend themselves to my mind as good, but in other matters I prefer judging for myself and following my own directions.' What would you do in such a case?" I asked.

"Do?" he replied with indignation. "Do? I would soon leave such a man as that to his own care. For, of course," he added, "I could do nothing for him unless he would put his whole case into my hands without any reserves and would obey my directions implicitly."

"It is necessary, then," I said, "for doctors to be obeyed, if they are to have any chance to cure their patients?"

"Implicitly obeyed!" was his emphatic reply.

"And that is consecration," I continued. "God must have the whole case put into His hands without any reserves, and His directions must be implicitly followed."

"I see it," he exclaimed. "I see it! And I will do it. God shall have His own way with me from now on."

An entire surrender of the whole being to God means that spirit, soul, and body are placed under His absolute control, for Him to do with us just what He pleases. We mean that the language of our hearts, under all circumstances and in view of every act, is to be "Thy will be done." We mean the giving up of all liberty of choice. We mean a life of inevitable obedience.

To a soul ignorant of God, this may look hard; but to those who know Him, it is the happiest and most restful of lives. He is our Father, and He loves us, and He knows just what is best, and therefore, of course, His will is the very most blessed thing that can come to us under any circumstances. But it really would seem as if God's own children were more afraid of His will than of anything else in life—His lovely, lovable will, which only means loving-kindnesses and tender mercies, and blessings unspeakable to their souls! I wish I could only show to everyone the unfathomable sweetness of the will of God. Heaven is a place of infinite bliss because His will is perfectly done there, and our lives share in this bliss just in proportion as His will is perfectly done in them. He loves us—*loves us*, I say—and the will of love is always blessing for its loved one. Could we but for one moment get a glimpse into the mighty depths of His love, our hearts would spring out to meet His will and embrace it as our richest treasure; and we would abandon ourselves to it with an enthusiasm of gratitude and joy that such a wondrous privilege could be ours.

A great many Christians seem practically to think that all their Father in heaven wants is a chance to make them miserable and to take away all their blessings; and they imagine, poor souls, that if they hold on to things in their own will, they can hinder Him from doing this.

A Christian lady who had this feeling was once expressing to a friend how impossible she found it to say, "Thy will be done," and how afraid she should be to do it. She was the mother of an only little boy, who was the heir to a great fortune and the idol of her heart.

After she had stated her difficulties fully, her friend said, "Suppose your little Charley should come running to you tomorrow and say, 'Mother, I have made up my mind to let you have your own way with me from this time forward. I am always going to obey you, and I want you to do just whatever you think best with me. I will trust your love.' How would you feel toward him? Would you say to yourself, 'Ah, now I shall have a chance to make Charley miserable. I will take away all his pleasures and fill his life with every hard and disagreeable thing that I can find. I will force him to do just the things that are the most difficult for him to do and will give him all sorts of impossible commands' "?

"Oh no no no!" exclaimed the indignant mother. "You know I would not. You know I would hug him to my heart and cover him with kisses and would hasten to fill his life with all that was sweetest and best."

"And are you tenderer and more loving than God?" asked her friend.

"Ah no!" was the reply. "I see my mistake. Of course I must not be any more afraid of saying, 'Thy will be done,' to my heavenly Father, than I would want Charley to be of saying it to me."

Faith is an absolutely necessary element in the reception of any gift. Let our friends give a thing to us wholeheartedly; it is not really ours until we believe it has been given and claim it as our own. Above all, this is true in gifts that are purely mental or spiritual. Love may be lavished upon us by another without stint or measure, but until we believe that we are loved, it never really becomes ours.

I suppose most Christians understand this principle in reference to the matter of their forgiveness. They know that the forgiveness of sins through Jesus might have been preached to them forever, but it would never really have become theirs until they believed this preaching and claimed the forgiveness as their own. But when it comes to living the Christian life, they lose sight of this principle and think that, having been saved by faith, they are now to live by works and efforts. Instead of continuing to *receive*, they now begin to *do*. This makes our declaration that the life hid with Christ in God is entered into by faith seem perfectly unintelligible to them. And yet it is plainly declared that "*as* ye have therefore received Christ Jesus the Lord, *so* walk ye in him." We received Him by faith, and by faith alone; therefore we are to walk in Him by faith and by faith alone. *Then* we believed that Jesus was our Savior from the guilt of sin, and according to our faith it was unto us. *Now* we must believe that He is our Savior from the power of sin, and according to our faith it shall be unto us. *Then* we trusted Him for forgiveness, and it became ours; *now* we must trust Him for righteousness, and it shall become ours also. *Then* we took Him as a Savior in the future from the penalties of our sins; *now* we must take Him as a Savior in the present from the bondage of our sins. *Then* He was our Redeemer; *now* He is our Life. *Then* He lifted us out of the pit; *now* He is to seat us in heavenly places with Himself.

God "hath blessed us with all spiritual blessings in heavenly places in Christ," but until we set the foot of faith upon them, they do not practically become ours. "According to our faith" is always the limit and the rule.

But this faith of which I am speaking must be a present faith. No faith that is exercised in the future tense amounts to anything. No faith that looks for a future deliverance from the power of sin will ever lead a soul into the life we are describing. Perhaps no four words in the language have more meaning in them than the following, which I would have you repeat over and over with your voice and with your soul, emphasizing each time a different word:

Jesus saves me now—It is He.

Jesus *saves* me now—It is His work to save.

Jesus saves *me* now—I am the one to be saved.

Jesus saves me *now*—He is doing it every moment.

To sum up, then: In order to enter into this blessed interior life of rest and triumph, you have two steps to take—first, entire abandonment, and second, absolute faith. No matter what may be the complications of your peculiar experience, no matter what your difficulties or your surroundings or your "peculiar temperament," these two steps, definitely taken and unwaveringly persevered in, will certainly bring you out sooner or later into the green pastures and still waters of this life hid with Christ in God. If you will let every other consideration go and simply devote your attention to these two points and be very clear and definite about them, your progress will be rapid, and your soul will reach its desired haven far sooner than you can now think possible.

A lady, now very eminent in this life of trust, when she was seeking in great darkness and perplexity to enter in, said to the friend who was trying to help her, "You all say, 'Abandon yourself and trust, abandon yourself and trust'; but I do not know how. I wish you would just do it out loud, so that I may see how you do it."

Shall I do it out loud for you?

"Lord Jesus, I believe You are able and willing to deliver me from all the care and unrest and bondage of my Christian life. I believe You died to set me free, not only in the future, but now and here. I believe You are stronger than sin, and that You canst keep me, even me, in my extreme of weakness, from falling into its snares or yielding obedience to its commands. And, Lord, I am going to trust You to keep me. I have tried keeping myself and have failed most grievously. I am absolutely helpless. So now I will trust You. I give myself to You. I keep back no reserves. Body, soul, and spirit, I present myself to You as a piece of clay to be fashioned into anything Your love and Your wisdom shall choose. And now I *am* Yours. I believe You accept that which I present to You; I believe that this poor, weak, foolish heart has been taken possession of by You, and that You have even at this very moment begun to work in me to will and to do of Your good pleasure. I trust You *utterly*, and I trust You *now*."

Are you afraid to take this step? Does it seem too sudden, too much like a leap in the dark? Do you not know that the step of faith always "falls on the seeming void, but finds the rock beneath"? If ever you are to enter this glorious land, flowing with milk and honey, you must sooner or later step into the brimming waters, for there is no other path; and to do it now may save you months and even years of disappointment and grief. Hear the word of the Lord: "Have not I commanded thee? Be strong and of a good courage; be not afraid, neither be thou dismayed: for the LORD thy God is with thee whithersoever thou goest."

PART II

Difficulties

CHAPTER 5

Difficulties Concerning Consecration

Christians should not be ignorant of the temptations that seem to stand ready to oppose every onward step of their progress heavenward and that are especially active when the soul is awakened to a hunger and thirst after righteousness and begins to reach out after the fullness that is ours in Christ.

The one chief temptation that meets the soul at this juncture is the same that assaults it all along the pathway, at every step of its progress; namely, the question as to *feelings*. Because we do not feel that God has taken us in hand, we cannot believe that He has. As usual, we put feeling first and faith second, and fact last of all. Now, God's invariable rule in everything is, fact first, faith second, and feeling last of all. The way to meet this temptation is to adopt His order by putting faith before feeling. Give yourself to the Lord definitely and fully, according to your present light, asking the Holy Spirit to show you all that is contrary to Him, either in your heart or life. If He shows you anything, give it to the Lord immediately, and say in reference to it, "Thy will be done." If He shows you nothing, then believe that there is nothing and conclude that you have given Him all. Then recognize that it must be the fact, that, when you give yourself to God, He accepts you; and at once let your faith take hold of this fact. If you are steadfast in this reckoning, sooner or later the feeling will come. Is this the way in which you have been acting toward God in this matter of consecration? You have given yourself to Him over and over daily, perhaps for months, but you have invariably come away from your seasons of consecration wondering whether you really have given yourself after all and whether He has taken you. And because you have not *felt* any change, you have concluded at last, after many painful tossings, that the thing has not been done. Do you know, dear believer, that this sort of perplexity will last forever unless you cut it short by faith? Come to the point of considering the matter an accomplished and settled thing, and leave it there before you can possibly expect any change of feeling whatever.

The Levitical law of offerings to the Lord settles this as a primary fact, that everything given to

Him becomes, by that very act, something holy, set apart from all other things, something that cannot without sacrilege be put to any other uses. The giver might have made his offering very grudgingly and halfheartedly, but, having made it, the matter was taken out of his hands altogether, and the devoted thing, by God's own law, became "most holy unto the Lord." It was not made holy by the state of mind of the giver but by the holiness of the divine receiver. All Israel would have been aghast at the man who, having once given his offering, should have reached out his hand to take it back. Yet, day after day, earnest-hearted Christians, with no thought of the sacrilege they are committing, are guilty in their own experience of a similar act, by giving themselves to the Lord in solemn consecration and then, through unbelief, taking back that which they have given.

Because God is not visibly present to the eye, it is difficult to feel that a transaction with Him is real. What we need, therefore, is to see that God's presence is a certain fact always, and that every act of our soul is done before Him, and that a word spoken in prayer is as really spoken to Him as if our eyes could see Him and our hands could touch Him. Then we shall cease to have such vague conceptions of our relations with Him and shall feel the binding force of every word we say in His presence.

I know some will say here, "Ah yes, but if He would only speak to me and say that He took me when I gave myself to Him, I would have no trouble then in believing it." No, of course you would not; but then where would be the room for faith? Sight is not faith, and hearing is not faith, neither is feeling faith; but believing when we cannot see, hear, or feel *is* faith; and everywhere the Bible tells us our salvation is by faith. Therefore we must believe before we feel, and often against our feelings, if we would honor God by our faith. It is always he who believes who has the witness, not he who doubts. When we surrender ourselves to the Lord, according to His own command, He does then and there receive us, and from that moment we are His. A real transaction has taken place that cannot be violated without dishonor on our part, and that we know will not be violated by Him.

In Deuteronomy 26:17–19, we see God's way of working under these circumstances. "Thou hast avouched the Lord this day to be thy God, and to walk in his ways, and to keep his statutes, and his commandments, and his judgments, and to hearken unto his voice: and the Lord hath avouched thee this day to be his peculiar people, as he hath promised thee, and that thou shouldest keep all his commandments. . .and that thou mayest be an holy people unto the Lord thy God, as he hath spoken."

When we declare the Lord our God and that we will walk in His ways and keep His commandments, He declares us to be His and that we *shall* keep all

His commandments. And from that moment He takes possession of us. This has always been His principle of working.

Look at a New Testament declaration that approaches the subject from a different side, but which settles it, I think, quite as definitely. It is in 1 John 5:14–15, and reads, "And this is the confidence that we have in him, that, if we ask anything according to his will, he heareth us: and if we know that he hear us, whatsoever we ask, we know that we have the petitions that we desired of him." Is it according to God's will that you should be entirely surrendered to Him? There can be, of course, but one answer to this, for He has *commanded* it. Therefore, on God's own word, you are obliged to know that He hears you. And knowing this much, you are compelled to go further and know that you have the petitions that you have desired of Him. That you *have*, I say—not will have, or may have, but have now in actual possession. It is thus that we "obtain promises" by faith. It is thus that we have "access by faith" into the grace that is given us in our Lord Jesus Christ. It is this way, and this way only, that we come to know our hearts "purified by faith" and are enabled to live by faith, to stand by faith, to walk by faith.

You have trusted the Lord Jesus for the forgiveness of your sins and know something of what it is to belong to the family of God and to be made an heir of God through faith in Christ. Now you feel the longing to be conformed to the image of your Lord. You know there must be an entire surrender of yourself to Him, that He may work in you all the good pleasure of His will. And you have tried over and over to do it but up until now without any apparent success. Come once more to Him, in a surrender of your whole self to His will, as complete as you know how to make it. Ask Him to reveal to you, by His Spirit, any hidden rebellion; and if He reveals nothing, then believe that there is nothing. You have wholly yielded yourself to the Lord, and from henceforth you do not in any sense belong to yourself. Never listen to a suggestion to the contrary. If the temptation comes to wonder whether you really have completely surrendered yourself, meet it with an assertion that you have. Do not even argue the matter. Repel any such idea instantly and with determination. You meant it then; you mean it now; you have really done it. Your emotions may clamor against the surrender, but your will must hold firm. It is your purpose God looks at, not your feelings about that purpose. And your purpose, or will, is therefore the only thing you need to attend to.

Believe that God takes that which you have surrendered and consider that it is His. There is nothing more for you to do, except to be from now on an obedient child, for you are the Lord's now, absolutely and entirely in His hands. He has undertaken the whole care and management and forming of you, and will, according to His Word, "work in you that which is well pleasing in his sight through Jesus Christ." If you begin to question your surrender or God's acceptance of it, then your wavering faith will produce a wavering experience. You will find it a great help to put your reckoning into words and say over and over to yourself and to your God, "Lord, I am Yours. I yield myself up entirely to You, and I believe that You accept me. I leave myself with You. Work in me all the good pleasure of Your will, and I will only lie still in Your hands and trust You."

Make this a daily, definite act of your will, and many times a day recur to it, as being your continual attitude before the Lord. Confess it to yourself. Confess it to your God. Confess it to your friends. Sooner or later, you will find that you are being made into "a holy people unto the LORD, as he hath spoken."

CHAPTER 6

Difficulties Concerning Faith

The next step after consecration in the soul's progress is that of faith. And here, as in the first step, the soul encounters at once certain forms of difficulty and hindrance.

The subject of faith is involved in such a hopeless mystery to his mind that this assertion, instead of throwing light upon the way of entrance, only seems to make it more difficult and involved than ever.

"Of course it is by faith," he says, "for I know that everything in the Christian life is by faith. But that is just what makes it so hard, for I have no faith, and I do not even know what it is nor how to get it." Baffled at the very outset by this insuperable difficulty, he is plunged into darkness and almost despair.

This trouble arises from the fact that the subject of faith is very generally misunderstood; for, in reality, faith is the simplest and plainest thing in the world and the easiest of exercise.

Your idea of faith is either a religious exercise of soul or an inward, gracious disposition of heart, something tangible. When you have secured it, you can look at and rejoice over it and use it as a passport to God's favor or a coin with which to purchase His gifts. And you have been praying for faith, expecting all the while to get something like this; and never having received any such thing, you are insisting upon it that you have no faith. Now faith, in fact, is not the least like this. It is nothing at all tangible. It is simply believing God. You see something and thus know that you have sight; you believe something and thus know that you have faith. For as sight is only seeing, so faith is only believing. If you believe the truth, you are saved; if you believe a lie, you are lost. Your salvation comes, not because your faith saves you, but because it links you to the Savior who saves.

Recognize, then, the extreme simplicity of faith—that it is nothing more nor less than just believing God when He says He either has done something for us or will do it; and then trusting Him to keep His word. What does it mean to trust another to do a piece of work for me? I can only answer that it means committing the work to that other and leaving it without anxiety in his hands.

All of us have many times trusted very important affairs to others in this way and have felt perfect rest in this trust because of the confidence we have had in those who have undertaken them.

How constantly do mothers trust their most precious infants to the care of babysitters and feel no shadow of anxiety! How continually we are all of us trusting our health and our lives, without a thought of fear, to cooks and coachmen, engine drivers, railway conductors, and all sorts of paid servants who have us completely at their mercy and who could, if they chose to do so, or even if they failed in the necessary carefulness, plunge us into misery or death in a moment. All this we do and make no demur about it. Upon the slightest acquaintance, often we thus put our trust in people, requiring only the general knowledge of human nature and the common rules of human intercourse as the foundation of our trust, and we never feel as if we were doing anything in the least remarkable.

Try to imagine yourself acting in your human relations as you do in your spiritual relations. When you sat down to breakfast, you would say, "I cannot eat anything on this table, for I have no faith, and I cannot believe the cook has not put poison into the coffee, or that the butcher has not sent home diseased or unhealthy meat," so you would go starving away. When you went out to your daily avocations, you would say, "I cannot ride in the railway train, for I have no faith, and therefore I cannot trust the engineer, nor the conductor, nor the builders of the carriages, nor the managers of the road." When your friends met you with any statements or your business agent with any accounts, you would say, "I am very sorry that I cannot believe you, but I have no faith and never can believe anybody." If you opened a newspaper, you would be forced to lay it down again, saying, "I really cannot believe a word this paper says, for I have no faith. I do not believe there is any such person as the queen, for I never saw her; nor any such country as Ireland, for I was never there. I have no faith, so of course I cannot believe anything that I have not actually felt and touched myself. It is a great trial, but I cannot help it, for I have no faith."

Just picture such utter folly. Ask yourself: If this want of faith in your fellowmen is so dreadful and such utter folly, what must it be when you tell God that you have no power to trust Him, nor believe His word; that it is a great trial, but you cannot help it, for you "have no faith"?

Is it possible that you can trust your fellowmen and cannot trust your God, that you can receive the "witness of men" and cannot receive the "witness of God," that you can believe man's records and cannot believe God's record, that you can commit your dearest earthly interests to your weak, failing fellow creatures without a fear and are afraid to commit your spiritual interests to the Savior who laid down

His life for you and of whom it is declared that He is "able also to save them to the uttermost that come unto God by him"?

You say, I cannot believe without the Holy Spirit. Very well; will you conclude, then, that your want of faith is because of the failure of the Holy Spirit to do His work? In taking up the position that you have no faith and cannot believe, you are not only "making God a liar," but you are also showing an utter want of confidence in the Holy Spirit.

God is always ready to help our infirmities. We never have to wait for Him; He is always waiting for us. And I for my part have such absolute confidence in the Holy Ghost and in His being always ready to do His work, that I dare to say to every one of you, that you *can* believe now, at this very moment. If you do not, it is not the Spirit's fault, but your own. Put your will, then, over on the believing side. Say, "Lord, I will believe; I do believe," and continue to say it. Insist upon believing in the face of every suggestion of doubt that intrudes itself. Out of your very unbelief, throw yourself unreservedly on the Word and promises of God, and dare to abandon yourself to the keeping and saving power of the Lord Jesus. If you have ever trusted a precious interest in the hands of an earthly friend, I entreat you, trust yourself and all your spiritual interest now in the hands of your heavenly Friend, and never, *never*, *never*, allow yourself to doubt again.

Remember always that there are two things that are more utterly incompatible even than oil and water, and these two are trust and worry. Would you call it trust if you should give something into the hands of a friend to attend to for you and then should spend your nights and days in anxious thought and worry as to whether it would be rightly and successfully done? And can you call it trust when you have given the saving and keeping of your soul into the hands of the Lord if day after day and night after night you are spending hours of anxious thought and questionings about the matter?

When a believer really trusts anything, he ceases to worry about the thing he has trusted. And when he worries, it is a plain proof that he does not trust. Tested by this rule, how little real trust there is in the church of Christ! No wonder our Lord asked the pathetic question, "When the Son of man cometh, shall he find faith on the earth?" He will find plenty of work, a great deal of earnestness, and doubtless many consecrated hearts; but shall He find faith, the one thing He values more than all the rest? I remember, very early in my Christian life, having every tender and loyal impulse within me stirred to the depths by an appeal I met within a volume of old sermons, to all who loved the Lord Jesus, that they should show to others how worthy He was of being trusted by the steadfastness of their own faith in Him. As I read the inspiring words, there came to me a sudden glimpse of the privilege and the glory of being called to walk in paths so dark that only an utter recklessness of trust would be possible!

You have trusted God in a few things, and He has not failed you. Trust Him now for everything, and see if He does not do for you exceeding abundantly above all that you could ever have asked or even thought, not according to your power or capacity, but according to His own mighty power, working in you all the good pleasure of His most blessed will.

It is not hard, you find, to trust the management of the universe and of all the outward creation to the Lord. Can your case then be so much more complex and difficult than these that you need to be anxious or troubled about His management of you? Away with such unworthy doubtings! Take your stand on the power and trustworthiness of your God, and see how quickly all difficulties will vanish before a steadfast determination to believe. It is a law of spiritual life that every act of trust makes the next act less difficult, until at length, if these acts are persisted in, trusting becomes, like breathing, the natural unconscious action of the redeemed soul.

Therefore put your will into your believing. Your faith must not be a passive imbecility but an active energy. You may have to believe against every appearance, but no matter. Set your face like a flint to say, "I will believe, and I know I shall not be destroyed." If you are a child of God at all, have at least as much faith as a grain of mustard seed, and therefore you dare not say again that you "cannot trust because you have no faith." Say rather, "I can trust my Lord, and I will trust Him. And none of the powers of earth or hell shall be able to make me doubt my wonderful, glorious, faithful Redeemer!"

Be patient and trustful, and wait. This time of darkness is only permitted that "the trial of your faith, being much more precious than of gold that perisheth, though it be tried with fire, might be found unto praise and honour and glory at the appearing of Jesus Christ."

CHAPTER 7

Difficulties Concerning the Will

When the child of God has, by entire abandonment and absolute trust, stepped out of himself into Christ and has begun to know something of the blessedness of the life hid with Christ in God, there is one form of difficulty that is especially likely to start up in his path. After the first emotions of peace and rest have somewhat subsided, or if, as is sometimes the case, they have never seemed to come at all, he begins to feel such an utter unreality in the things he has been passing through that he seems to himself like a hypocrite when he says or even thinks they are real. It seems to him that his belief does not go below the surface, that it is a mere lip-belief and therefore of no account, and that his surrender is not a surrender of the heart and therefore cannot be acceptable to God. He is afraid to say he is altogether the Lord's, for fear he will be telling an untruth; and yet he cannot bring himself to say he is not.

But there is nothing here that isn't easily overcome when the Christian once thoroughly understands the principles of the new life and has learned *how* to live in it. The common thought is that this life hid with Christ in God is lived in the emotions, and consequently all the attention of the soul is directed toward them. Because emotions are satisfactory or otherwise, the soul rests or is troubled. Now the truth is that this life is not lived in the emotions at all but in the will. Therefore, if man's will is kept steadfastly abiding in its center, God's will, the varying states of emotion do not in the least disturb or affect the reality of the life.

Fenelon says that "pure religion resides in the will alone." By this he means that, as the will is the governing power in the man's nature, if the will is set right, all the rest of the nature must come into harmony. The will is the deliberate choice, the deciding power, to which all that is in the man must yield obedience.

It is sometimes thought that the emotions are the governing power in our nature. But I think all of us know, as a matter of practical experience, that there is an independent self within us, behind our emotions and behind our wishes, that decides everything and controls everything. Our emotions belong to us and are put up with and enjoyed by us, but they are not our true selves. If God is to take possession of us, it must be into this central will or personality that He enters. If, then, He is reigning there by the power of His Spirit, all the rest of our nature must come under His sway, and as the will is, so is the man.

A young man of great intelligence, seeking to enter into this new life, was utterly discouraged at finding himself the slave to a chronic habit of doubting. Nothing seemed real or true to his emotions. The more he struggled, the more unreal it all became. Someone told him this secret concerning the will: that if he would only put his will over on the believing side, if he would choose to believe, he need not then trouble about his emotions, for they would find themselves compelled, sooner or later, to come into harmony.

"What!" he said. "Do you mean to tell me that I can *choose* to believe in that bold way, when nothing seems true to me? Will that kind of believing be real?"

"Yes," was the answer. "Simply put your will over on God's side, making up your mind that you will believe what He says because He says it." The young man paused a moment and then said solemnly, "I understand and will do what you say. I cannot control my emotions, but I can control my will. The new life begins to look possible to me, if it is only my will that needs to be set straight in the matter. I can give my will to God, and I do."

From that moment, disregarding all the pitiful clamoring of his emotions, which continually accused him of being a wretched hypocrite, this young man held on steadily to the decision of his will, answering every accusation with the continued assertion that he chose to believe, he meant to believe, he did believe, until at the end of a few days he found himself triumphant, with every emotion and every thought brought into captivity to the power of the Spirit of God. At times it drained all the willpower he possessed to his lips, to say that he believed, so contrary was it to all the evidence of his senses or of his emotions. But he caught the idea that his will was, after all, himself, and that if he kept that on God's side, he was doing all he could do. God alone could change his emotions or control his being. The result has been one of the grandest Christian lives I know of in its marvelous simplicity, directness, and power over sin.

A lady who had entered into this life hid with Christ was confronted by a great prospective trial. But she had learned this secret of the will, and knowing that, at the bottom, she herself did really choose the will of God for her portion, she did not pay the slightest attention to her emotions but persisted in meeting every thought concerning the trial with the words, repeated over and over, "Thy will be done! Thy will be done!" In an incredibly short space of time, every thought was brought into captivity, and she began to find even her very emotions rejoicing in the will of God.

Again, there was a lady who had a besetting sin. But she learned this secret concerning the will, and going to her closet, she said, "Lord, You see that with my emotions I love this sin, but in my real central self I hate it. Until now my emotions have had the mastery; but now I put my will into Your hands and give it up to Your working. I will never again consent in my will to yield to this sin. Take possession of my will and work in me to will and to do of Thy good pleasure." Immediately she began to find deliverance.

How do you apply this principle to your difficulties? Cease to consider your emotions, for they are only the servants. Simply regard your will, which is the real king in your being. Is that given up to God? Is that put into His hands? Does your will decide to believe? Does your will choose to obey? If this is the case, then *you* are in the Lord's hands, and you decide to believe, and you choose to obey; for your will is yourself. Get hold of this secret and discover that you can ignore your emotions and simply pay attention to the state of your will. Scripture commands you to yield yourself to God, to present yourself a living sacrifice to Him, to abide in Christ, to walk in the light, to die to self. When this feeling of unreality or hypocrisy comes, do not be troubled by it. It is only in your emotions, and it is not worth a moment's thought. Only see to it that your will is in God's hands, that your inward self is abandoned to His working, that your choice, your decision, is on His side, and leave it there.

The will is like a wise mother in a nursery. The feelings are like a set of clamoring, crying children. The mother, knowing that she is the authority figure, pursues her course lovingly and calmly in spite of all their clamors. The result is that the children are sooner or later won over to the mother's course of action and fall in with her decisions, and all is harmonious and happy. But if that mother should for a moment let in the thought that the children were the masters instead of herself, confusion would reign unchecked. In how many souls at this very moment is there nothing but confusion, simply because the feelings are allowed to govern instead of the will?

The real thing in your experience is what your will decides, not your emotions. You are far more in danger of hypocrisy and untruth in yielding to the assertions of your feelings than in holding fast to the decision of your will. I am convinced that throughout the Bible the verses concerning the "heart" do not mean the emotions, that which we now understand by the word *heart*. They mean the will, the personality of the man, the man's own central self. The object of God's dealing with man is that this "I" may be yielded up to Him and this central life abandoned to His entire control. It is not the feelings of the man

God wants, but the man himself.

Do not let us make a mistake here. I say we must "give up" our wills, but I do not mean we are to be left will-less. We are not so to give up our wills as to be left like limp, nerveless creatures, without any will at all. We are simply to substitute the higher, divine, mature will of God for our foolish, misdirected wills of ignorance and immaturity. Is your face set as a flint to will what God wills? He wills that you should be entirely surrendered to Him and that you should trust Him perfectly. If you have taken the steps of surrender and faith in your will, it is your right to believe that no matter how much your feelings may clamor against it, you *are* all the Lord's, and He *has* begun to "work in you both to will and to do of His good pleasure."

The following letter is a remarkable, practical illustration of this chapter's teaching. Pasteur Theodore Monod of Paris handed it to me. It details the experience of a Presbyterian minister:

Newburgh, Sept. 26, 1842
Dear Brother,—Since I last saw you, I have been pressing forward, and yet there has been nothing remarkable in my experience of which I can speak. Indeed, I do not know that it is best to look for remarkable things. Instead, we should strive to be holy, as God is holy, pressing right on toward the mark of the prize.

The Lord deals differently with different souls,

and we shouldn't attempt to copy the experience of others. Yet everyone who is seeking after a clean heart should pay attention to certain things.

There must be a personal consecration of all to God, a covenant made with God that we will be wholly and forever. I pledged myself to the Lord and laid my all upon the altar, a living sacrifice, to the best of my ability. After I rose from my knees, I was painfully conscious that there was no change in my feelings. But yet I was sure that I had, with all the sincerity and honesty of purpose of which I was capable, made an entire and eternal consecration of myself to God. I did not then consider the work as done by any means, but I determined to abide in a state of complete devotion to God, a living perpetual sacrifice. And now came the effort to do this.

I knew also that I must believe that God accepted me and dwelled in my heart. I was conscious I did not believe this, and yet I desired to do so. I read with much prayer John's first epistle and endeavored to assure my heart of God's love to me as an individual. I finally hit upon the method of living by the moment, and then I found rest.

I felt shut up to a momentary dependence upon the grace of Christ. I would not permit the adversary to trouble me about the past or future. I agreed that I would be a child of Abraham and walk by naked faith in the

Word of God and not by inward feelings and emotions. I sought to be a Bible Christian. Since that time the Lord has given me a steady victory over sins which before enslaved me. I have covenanted to walk by faith and not by feelings.

Your fellow-soldier,
William Hill

CHAPTER 8

Difficulties Concerning Guidance

You have now begun the life of faith. You have given yourself to the Lord to be His wholly and completely, and you are now entirely in His hands to be molded and fashioned according to His own divine purpose into a vessel unto His honor. Your one most earnest desire is to follow Him wherever He may lead you and to be very pliable in His hands. You are trusting Him to "work in you both to will and to do of His good pleasure." But you find a great difficulty here. You have not yet learned to know the voice of the Good Shepherd and are therefore in great doubt and perplexity as to what really is His will concerning you.

There is a way out of all these difficulties to

the fully surrendered soul. The first thing is to be sure that you really do *purpose* to obey the Lord in every respect. If this is your purpose and your soul only needs to know the will of God in order to consent to it, then you surely cannot doubt His willingness to make His will known and to guide you in the right paths. There are many very clear promises in reference to this:

John 10:3–4: " 'He calleth his own sheep by name, and leadeth them out. And when he putteth forth his own sheep, he goeth before them, and the sheep follow him: for they know his voice.' "

John 14:26: " 'But the Comforter, which is the Holy Ghost, whom the Father will send in my name, he shall teach you all things, and bring all things to your remembrance, whatsoever I have said unto you.' "

James 1:5–6: "If any of you lack wisdom, let him ask of God, that giveth to all men liberally, and upbraideth not; and it shall be given him."

Our faith must confidently look for and expect God's guidance. This is essential, for in James 1:6–7, we are told, "Let him ask in faith, nothing wavering. For he that wavereth is like a wave of the sea driven with the wind and tossed. For let not that man think that he shall receive any thing of the Lord." God promises His divine guidance, and if you seek it, you are sure to receive it.

Next, remember that our God has all knowledge and all wisdom and that it is very possible He may guide you into paths wherein *He* knows great blessings are awaiting you. Nevertheless, to the shortsighted human eyes around you, everything seems to result in confusion and loss. His very love for you may perhaps lead you to run counter to the loving wishes of even your dearest friends. Luke 14:26–33 and similar passages state that in order to be a disciple and follower of your Lord, you may perhaps be called upon to forsake inwardly all that you have—father or mother, or brother or sister, or husband or wife, or maybe your own life. Unless the possibility of this is clearly recognized, you will very likely get into difficulty, because it often happens that the child of God who enters upon this life of obedience is sooner or later led into paths that meet with the disapproval of those he loves best. Unless he is prepared for this and can trust the Lord through it all, he will scarcely know what to do.

How does God's guidance come to us? And how do we know His voice? There are four ways in which He reveals His will to us—through the scriptures, through providential circumstances, through the convictions of our own higher judgment, and through the inward impressions of the Holy Spirit on our minds. Where these four harmonize, it is safe to say that God speaks.

If God tells me in one voice to do or to leave anything undone, He cannot possibly tell me the opposite in another voice. Therefore my rule for distinguishing the voice of God is to bring it to the test of this harmony.

The scriptures come first. If you are in doubt upon any subject, you must, first of all, consult the Bible about it and see whether there is any law there to direct you. Until you have found and obeyed God's will as it is there revealed, you must not ask nor expect a separate, direct, personal revelation. Where our Father has written out for us a plain direction about anything, He will not of course make a special revelation to us about that thing. And if we fail to search out and obey the scripture rule, where there is one, and look instead for an inward voice, we open ourselves to delusions and almost inevitably get into error. The Bible does not always give a rule for every particular course of action, and in these cases we need and must expect guidance in other ways. But the scriptures are far more explicit, even about details, than most people think, and there are not many important affairs in life for which a clear direction may not be found in God's book.

If, therefore, you find yourself in perplexity, first of all search and see whether the Bible speaks on the point in question, asking God to make plain to you, by the power of His Spirit, through the scriptures, what is His mind. And whatever shall seem to you plainly taught there, obey. No special guidance will ever be given about a point on which the scriptures are explicit, nor could any guidance ever be contrary to the scriptures.

Remember that the Bible is a book of principles and not a book of disjointed aphorisms. Isolated texts can be made to give approval to things to which the principles of scripture are totally opposed.

If, however, upon searching the Bible you do not find any principles that will settle your special point of difficulty, then seek guidance in the other ways mentioned, and God will surely voice Himself to you, by a conviction of your judgment, by providential circumstances, or by a clear inward impression. If any one of these tests fails, it is not safe to proceed, but wait in quiet trust until the Lord shows you the point of harmony, which He surely will, sooner or later, if it is His voice that is speaking. Anything that is out of this divine harmony must be rejected as not coming from God.

Never forget that "impressions" can come from other sources as well as from the Holy Spirit. The strong personalities of those around us are the source of a great many of our impressions. Impressions also arise often from our wrong physical conditions, which color things far more than we dream. And finally, impressions come from spiritual enemies. These spiritual enemies, whoever or whatever they may be, must by necessity communicate with us by means of our spiritual faculties, so their voices will be, as the voice of God is, an inward impression made upon our spirits. It is not enough to have a "leading." We must find out the source of that leading before we give ourselves up to follow it. It is not enough, either, for the leading to be very "remarkable," or the coincidences to be very striking, to stamp it as being surely from God. In all ages of the world, evil and deceiving agencies have been able to work miracles, foretell events, reveal secrets, and give "signs." And God's people have always been emphatically warned about being deceived thereby.

It is essential, therefore, that our "leadings" should all be tested by the teachings of scripture. But this alone is not enough. They must be tested as well by our own spiritually enlightened judgment or what is familiarly called "common sense."

Some, however, may say here, "But I thought we were not to depend on our human understanding in divine things." We are not to depend on our unenlightened human understanding but upon our human judgment and common sense enlightened by the Spirit of God. That is, God will speak to us through the abilities He has Himself given us and not independently of them. The third test to which our impressions must be brought is that of providential circumstances. If a "leading" is of God, the way will always open for it. Our Lord assures us of this when He says, in John 10:4, "And when he putteth forth his own sheep, *he goeth before them*, and the sheep *follow* him: for they know his voice." Notice here the expressions "goeth before" and "follow." He goes before to open a way, and we are to follow in the way He opens. It is never a sign of a divine leading when the Christian insists on opening his own way and riding roughshod over all opposing things. If the Lord "goes before" us, He will open the door for us, and we shall not need to batter down doors for ourselves.

The fourth point is that just as our impressions must be tested, as I have shown, by the other three voices, so must these other voices be tested by our inward impressions. If we feel a "stop in our minds" about anything, we must wait until that is removed before acting. A Christian who had advanced with unusual rapidity in the divine life gave me, as her secret, this simple direction: "I always mind the checks." We must not ignore the voice of our inward impressions. When the spiritual world is opened to a soul, both the good and the evil there will meet it. But we must not be discouraged by this. With the four tests I have mentioned and a divine sense of "oughtness" derived from the harmony of all of God's voices, there is nothing to fear. And to me it seems that the blessedness and joy of this direct communication of God's will to us is one of our grandest privileges. That God *cares* enough about us to desire to regulate the details of our lives is the strongest proof of love

He could give. God's law, therefore, is only another name of God's love; and the more minutely that law descends into the details of our lives, the surer we are made of the depth and reality of the love. We can never know the full joy and privileges of the life hid with Christ in God until we have learned the lesson of daily and hourly guidance.

God's promise is that He will work in us to *will* as well as to do of His good pleasure. This means, of course, that He will take possession of our will and work it for us. His suggestions will come to us, not so much as commands from the outside as desires springing up within. This makes it a service of perfect liberty. It is always easy to do what we desire to do, no matter how difficult the accompanying circumstances may be. He "writes his laws on our hearts and on our minds," so that our affection and our understanding embrace them, and we are *drawn* to obey instead of being *driven* to it.

It sometimes happens, however, that, in spite of all our efforts to discover the truth, the divine sense of "oughtness" does not seem to come, and our doubts and perplexities continue unenlightened. In such a case there is nothing to do but to wait until the light comes. But we must wait in faith and in an attitude of entire surrender, saying a continual yes to the will of our Lord, let it be what it may. If the suggestion is from Him, it will continue and strengthen; if it is not from

Him, it will disappear. If it continues, if every time we are brought into close communion with the Lord it seems to return, if it troubles us in our moments of prayer and disturbs all our peace, and if it conforms to the test of the divine harmony, we may then feel sure it is from God, and we must yield to it or suffer an unspeakable loss.

In all doubtful things stand still and refrain from action until God gives you light to know more clearly His mind concerning them. Very often you will find that the doubt has been His voice calling you to come into more perfect conformity to His will. But sometimes these doubtful things are only temptations, or morbid feelings, to which it would be most unwise for you to yield. The only safe way is to wait until you can act in faith, for "whatsoever is not of faith is sin."

Take all your present perplexities, then, to the Lord. Tell Him you only want to know and obey His voice, and ask Him to make it plain to you. Promise Him that you will obey, whatever it may be. Believe implicitly that He is guiding you according to His Word. In all doubtful things, wait for clear light. Look and listen for His voice continually. And the moment you are sure of it, then, but not until then, yield an immediate obedience. Trust Him to make you forget the impression if it is not His will. And if it continues and is in harmony with all His other voices, do not be afraid to obey.

Above everything else, trust Him. Nowhere is faith more needed than here. He has promised to guide. You have asked Him to do it. And now believe that He does, and take what comes as being His guidance. No earthly parent or master could guide his children or servants if they should refuse to take his commands as being really the expression of his will. And God *cannot* guide those souls who never trust Him enough to believe that He is doing it.

Above all, do not be afraid of this blessed life, lived hour by hour and day by day under the guidance of your Lord! If He seeks to bring you out of the world and into very close conformity to Himself, do not shrink from it. It is your most blessed privilege. Rejoice in it. Embrace it eagerly. Let everything go that it may be yours.

CHAPTER 9

Difficulties Concerning Doubts

A great many Christians are slaves to a chronic habit of doubting. I do not mean doubts as to the existence of God or the truths of the Bible, but doubts as to their own personal relations with the God in whom they profess to believe, doubts as to the forgiveness of their sins, doubts as to their hopes of heaven, and doubts about their own inward experience. Their lives are made wretched, their usefulness is effectually hindered, and their communion with God is continually broken by their doubts.

Many of us remember our childish fascination, and yet horror, in the story of Christian's imprisonment in Doubting Castle by the wicked giant Despair and our exultant sympathy in his escape through those massive gates and from the cruel tyrant. Little did we suspect then that we should ever find ourselves taken prisoner by the same giant and imprisoned in the same castle. But I fear that each one of us, if we were perfectly honest, would have to confess to at least one such experience and some of us perhaps to a great many.

It seems strange that people, whose very name of believers implies that their one chief characteristic is that they believe, should have to confess that they have doubts. And yet it is such a universal habit that if the name were to be given over again, the only fitting and descriptive name that could be given to many of God's children would have to be that of doubters. In fact, most Christians have settled down under their doubts as to a sort of inevitable malady from which they suffer acutely but to which they must try to be resigned as a part of the necessary discipline of this earthly life; and they lament over their doubts as a man might lament over his rheumatism, making themselves out as "interesting cases" of special and peculiar trial, which require the tenderest sympathy and the utmost consideration.

This is too often true even of believers who are earnestly longing to enter upon the life and walk of faith and who have made, perhaps, many steps toward it. They may have gotten rid of the old doubts that once tormented them—whether their sins are really forgiven and whether they shall, after all, get safe to heaven—but they have not gotten rid of doubting. They have simply shifted the habit to a higher platform. This includes an interminable array of doubts concerning most of the declarations and promises our Father has made to His children. One after another they fight with these promises and refuse to believe them until they can have some more reliable proof of their being true than the simple word of their God; and then they wonder why they are permitted to walk in such darkness and look upon themselves almost in the light of martyrs and groan under the peculiar spiritual conflicts they are compelled to endure.

Doubts would be better named spiritual rebellions! Our fight is a fight of faith; and the moment we let in doubts, our fight ceases and our rebellion begins.

To drunkards and doubters alike, I would dare to do nothing else but proclaim the perfect deliverance which the Lord Jesus Christ has in store for them. I would beseech, entreat, and beg them, with all the power at my command, to avail themselves of that deliverance and be free from the bonds of their sin. In the sight of God, I truly believe doubting is in some cases as displeasing as lying. It certainly is more dishonoring to Him, for it attacks His truthfulness and defames His character. John says that "he that believeth not God hath made him a liar," and it seems to me that hardly anything could be worse than thus to fasten on God the character of being a liar! Have you ever thought of this as the result of your doubting?

I remember seeing once the indignation and sorrow of a mother's heart deeply stirred by a little doubting on the part of one of her children. She had brought two little girls to my house to leave them while she did some errands. One of them, with the happy confidence of childhood, abandoned herself to all the pleasures she could find in my nursery and sang and played until her mother's return. The other one, with the wretched caution and mistrust of maturity, sat down alone in a corner to wonder, first, whether her mother would remember to come back for her and to fear she would be forgotten and then to imagine her mother would be glad of the chance to get rid of her anyhow because she was such a naughty girl. She ended with working herself up into a perfect frenzy of despair. I shall not easily forget the look on that mother's face when upon her return the weeping little girl told what was the matter with her. Grief, wounded love, indignation, and pity all strove together for mastery, and the mother hardly knew who was most at fault, herself or the child, that such doubts should be possible.

Have you ever indulged in hard thoughts against those who have, as you think, injured you? Have you ever brooded over their unkindnesses, pried into their malice, and imagined all sorts of wrong and uncomfortable things about them? It made you wretched, of course; but it is a fascinating sort of wretchedness that you could not easily give up.

The luxury of doubting is very similar. Things have gone wrong with you in your experience. Your temptations have been strange. Your "case" is different from others. What is more natural than to conclude that for some reason God has forsaken you and does not love you and is indifferent to your welfare? How irresistible is the conviction that you are too wicked for Him to care for or too difficult for Him to manage! You do not mean to blame Him or accuse Him of injustice, for you feel that His indifference and rejection of you are, because of your unworthiness, fully deserved. Although you think it is yourself you are doubting, you are really doubting the Lord and are indulging in as hard and wrong thoughts of Him as ever you did of a human enemy. For He declares that He came to save, not the righteous, but sinners; and your very sinfulness and unworthiness, instead of being a reason why He should not love you and care for you, are really your chief claim upon His love and His care.

He says, "What man of you, having an hundred sheep, if he lose one of them, doth not leave the ninety and nine in the wilderness, and go after that which is lost, until he find it?" Any thoughts of Him, therefore, that are different from this that

He Himself has said, are hard thoughts; and to indulge in them is far worse than to indulge in hard thoughts of any earthly friend or foe. From beginning to end of your Christian life it is always sinful to indulge in doubts. Doubts and discouragements are all from an evil source and are always untrue. A direct and emphatic denial is the only way to meet them.

Deliverance from the bondage of doubting must be by the same means as the deliverance from any other sin. It is found in Christ, and in Him alone. Hand your doubting over to Him as you have learned to hand your other temptations. I believe the only effectual remedy is to take a pledge against it, as you would urge a drunkard to do against drink, trusting in the Lord alone to keep you steadfast.

Like any other sin, the stronghold is in the will, and the will or purpose to doubt must be surrendered exactly as you surrender the will or purpose to yield to any other temptation. God always takes possession of a surrendered will. And if we come to the point of saying that we will not doubt and surrender this central fortress of our nature to Him, His blessed Spirit will begin at once to "work in us all the good pleasure of His will," and we shall find ourselves kept from doubting by His mighty and overcoming power.

The liberty to doubt must be given up forever; and we must consent to a continuous life of inevitable trust. Make a definite transaction of this surrender of doubting and come to a point about it. It will not do to give it up by degrees. The total-abstinence principle is the only effectual one here.

Then, the surrender once made, rest absolutely upon the Lord for deliverance in each time of temptation. The moment the assault comes, lift up the shield of faith against it. Hand the very first suggestion of doubt over to the Lord and let Him manage it. Refuse to entertain the doubt a single moment. Do not stop to argue out the matter with yourself or with your doubts. Pay no attention to them whatever, but treat them with the utmost contempt. Shut your door in their very face, and emphatically deny every word they say to you. Then let the doubts clamor as they may. They cannot hurt you if you will not let them in.

Often it has happened to me to find, on awaking in the morning, a perfect army of doubts clamoring at my door for admittance. I have been compelled to lift up the "shield of faith" the moment I have become conscious of these suggestions of doubt, and handing the whole army over to the Lord to conquer, I have begun to assert, over and over, my faith in Him, in the simple words, "God *is* my Father; I *am* His forgiven child; He *does* love me; Jesus saves me; Jesus saves me now!" The victory is always complete. The enemy has come in like a flood, but the "Spirit of the Lord has lifted up a standard against him," and my doubts have been put to flight. Dear doubting souls, go and do likewise, and a similar victory shall be yours. No earthly father has ever declared or shown his fatherhood a fraction as unmistakably or as lovingly as your heavenly Father has declared and shown His. If you would not "make God a liar," therefore, make your believing as inevitable and necessary a thing as your obedience. You would obey God, I believe, even though you should die in the act. Believe Him, also, even though the effort to believe should cost you your life. The conflict may be very severe; it may seem at times unendurable. But let your unchanging declaration be from this point on, "Though He slay me, yet will I trust in Him." When doubts come, meet them, not with arguments, but with affirmations of faith. All doubts are an attack of the enemy. The Holy Spirit never suggests them, never. He is the comforter, not the accuser; and He never shows us our need without at the same time revealing the divine supply.

Turn from them with horror, as you would from blasphemy, for they *are* blasphemy. You cannot, perhaps, hinder the suggestions of doubt from coming to you, any more than you can hinder the boys in the street from swearing as you go by. Just as you can refuse to listen to the boys or join in their oaths, so you can also refuse to listen to the doubts or join in with them. Write out your determination never to doubt again. Make it a real transaction between your soul and the Lord. Give up your liberty to doubt forever. Put your will in this matter over on the Lord's side, and trust Him to keep you from falling. Tell Him all about your utter weakness and your long-encouraged habits of doubt, and how helpless you are before it, and commit the whole battle to Him. Tell Him you *will* not doubt again, putting forth all your willpower on His side, and against His enemy and yours. Then, from now on, keep your face steadfastly "looking unto Jesus," away from yourself and away from your doubts, holding fast the profession of your faith without wavering, because "He is faithful that hath promised." Rely on *His* faithfulness, not on your own. You have committed the keeping of your soul to Him as unto a "faithful creator," and never again admit the possibility of His being unfaithful. Sooner or later you will come to *know* that it is true, and all doubts will vanish in the blaze of the glory of the absolute faithfulness of God!

Doubts and discouragements are, I believe, inlets by which evil enters, while faith is an impregnable wall against all evil.

Deliverance lies at your door. Try my plan, I beseech you, and see if it will not be true, that "according to your faith" it shall inevitably be unto you.

CHAPTER 10

Difficulties Concerning Temptations

Certain great mistakes are made concerning this matter of temptation in the practical working out of the life of faith.

First of all, people seem to expect that after the soul has entered into salvation through Christ, temptations will cease; and they think that the promised deliverance is to be not only from yielding to temptation but even also from being tempted. Next, they make the mistake of looking upon temptation as sin and of blaming themselves for suggestions of evil, even while they abhor them. This brings them into condemnation and discouragement. And continued discouragement always ends at last in actual sin. Sin makes an easy

Hannah Whitall Smith

prey of a discouraged soul, so that we fall often from the very fear of having fallen.

To meet the first of these difficulties, it is only necessary to refer to the scripture declarations that state that the Christian life is to be throughout a warfare. It is to be especially so when we are "seated in heavenly places in Christ Jesus" and are called to wrestle against spiritual enemies, whose power and skill to tempt us must doubtless be far superior to any we have ever encountered before. When the children of Israel first left Egypt, the Lord did not lead them through the country of the Philistines, although that was the nearest way. "For God said, 'Lest peradventure the people repent when they see war, and they return to Egypt.'" But afterward, when they had learned how to trust Him better, He permitted their enemies to attack them. Moreover, even in their wilderness journey they met with but few enemies and fought but few battles compared to those they encountered in the land of Canaan, where they found seven great nations and thirty-one kings to conquer, besides taking walled cities and overcoming giants.

They could not fight until they went into the land where these enemies were. The very power of your temptations may perhaps be one of the strongest proofs that you really are in the land of promise you have been seeking to enter because they are temptations peculiar to that land.

90

Consequently, never allow them to cause you to question the fact of your having entered it.

The second mistake is not quite so easy to deal with. It seems hardly worthwhile to say that temptation is not sin, and yet much distress arises from not understanding this fact. It is the enemy's grand ruse for entrapping us. He comes and whispers suggestions of evil to us—doubts, blasphemies, jealousies, envyings, and pride—and then turns round and says, "Oh, how wicked you must be to think such things! It is very plain that you are not trusting the Lord, for if you had been, it would be impossible for these things to have entered your heart."

This reasoning sounds so very plausible that we often accept it as true and so come under condemnation and are filled with discouragement. Then it is easy for temptation to develop into actual sin. One of the most fatal things in the life of faith is discouragement. One of the most helpful is confidence. A very wise man once said that in overcoming temptations confidence was the first thing, confidence the second, and confidence the third. We must *expect* to conquer. That is why the Lord said so often to Joshua, "Be strong and of good courage." "Be not afraid, neither be thou dismayed." "Only be thou strong and very courageous." And it is also the reason He says to us, "Let not your heart be troubled, neither let it be afraid." The power of temptation is in the fainting of our own hearts. The enemy knows this well, and he always begins his assaults by discouraging us, if he can in any way accomplish it.

This discouragement arises sometimes from what we think is a righteous grief and disgust at ourselves that such things *could* be any temptation to us but which is really mortification coming from the fact that we have been indulging in a secret self-congratulation that our tastes were too pure or our separation from the world was too complete for such things to tempt us. This mortification and discouragement, though they present an appearance of true humility, are really a far worse condition than the temptation itself, for they are nothing but the results of wounded self-love. True humility can bear to see its own utter weakness and foolishness revealed because it never expected anything from itself and knows that its only hope and expectation must be in God. Therefore, instead of discouraging the humble soul from trusting, such revelations drive it to a deeper and more complete trust. But the counterfeit humility that self-love produces plunges the soul into the depths of a faithless discouragement and drives it into the very sin with which it is so distressed.

An allegory illustrates this wonderfully. Satan called together a council of his servants to consult how they might make a good man sin.

One evil spirit started up and said, "I will make

him sin."

"How will you do it?" asked Satan.

"I will set before him the pleasures of sin," was the reply. "I will tell him of its delights and the rich rewards it brings."

"Ah," said Satan, "that will not do. He has tried it and knows better than that."

Then another imp started up and said, "I will make him sin."

"What will you do?" asked Satan.

"I will tell him of the pains and sorrows of virtue. I will show him that virtue has no delights and brings no rewards."

"Ah no!" exclaimed Satan. "That will not do at all, for he has tried it and knows that 'Wisdom's ways *are* ways of pleasantness, and all her paths are peace.'"

"Well," said another imp, starting up, "I will undertake to make him sin."

"And what will you do?" asked Satan, again.

"I will discourage his soul," was the short reply.

"Ah, that will do!" cried Satan. "That will do! We shall conquer him now."

But if we fail to recognize the truth about temptation, fleeing from discouragement is impossible. If the temptations are our own fault, we cannot help being discouraged. But they are not. The Bible says, "Blessed is the man that endureth temptation," and we are exhorted to "count it all joy when we fall into divers temptations." Temptation, therefore, cannot be sin. The truth is, it is no more a sin to hear these whispers and suggestions of evil in our souls than it is for us to hear the wicked talk of bad men as we pass along the street. The sin comes, in either case, only by our stopping and joining in with them.

A dear lady once came to me under great darkness, simply from not understanding this. She had been living very happily in the life of faith for some time and had been so free from temptation as almost to begin to think she would never be tempted again. She had lived a very sheltered, innocent life, and these thoughts seemed so awful to her that she felt she must be one of the most wicked of sinners to be capable of having them. She began by thinking that she could not possibly have entered into the rest of faith and ended by concluding that she had never been born again. I told her that these dreadful thoughts were purely and simply temptations, and that she herself was not to blame for them at all. She could not help them any more than she could help hearing if a wicked man should pour out his blasphemies in her presence. And I urged her to recognize and treat them as temptations only and not to blame herself or be discouraged but rather to turn at once to the Lord and commit them to Him. She grasped the truth, and the next time these blasphemous thoughts came, she said inwardly to the enemy, "I have found you out now. It is you who are suggesting these dreadful thoughts to me, and I hate them and will have nothing to do with them. The Lord is my helper. Take them to Him and settle them in His presence." Immediately the baffled enemy, finding himself discovered, fled in confusion, and her soul was perfectly delivered.

Another great mistake about temptations is in thinking that all time spent in combating them is lost. Hours pass, and we seem to have made no progress because we have been so beset with temptations. But it often happens that we have been serving God far more truly during these hours than in our times of comparative freedom from temptation. For we are fighting our Lord's battles when we are fighting temptation, and hours are often worth days to us under these circumstances. We read, "Blessed is the man that *endureth* temptation." Nothing so cultivates the grace of patience as the endurance of temptation, and nothing so drives the soul to an utter dependence upon the Lord Jesus as its continuance. And finally, nothing brings more praise and honor and glory to our Lord Himself than the trial of our faith that comes through manifold temptations. We cannot wonder, therefore, any longer at the exhortation with which the Holy Spirit opens the book of James: "Count it all joy when ye fall into divers temptations; knowing this, that the trying of your faith worketh patience. But let patience have her perfect work, that ye may be perfect and entire, wanting nothing."

The way of victory over temptation is by faith. We have discovered our own utter helplessness and know that we cannot do anything for ourselves. And we have learned that our only way, therefore, is to hand the temptation over to our Lord and trust Him to conquer it for us. But when we put it into His hands, we must *leave* it there. It seems impossible to believe that the Lord can or will manage our temptations without our help. To go on patiently "enduring" the continuance of a temptation without yielding to it and also without snatching ourselves out of the Lord's hands in regard to it is a wonderful victory for our impatient natures, but it is a victory we must gain if we would do what will please God.

We must then commit ourselves to the Lord for victory over our temptations, as we committed ourselves at first for forgiveness. And we must leave ourselves just as utterly in His hands for one as for the other.

Thousands of God's children have done this and can testify today that marvelous victories have been gained for them over numberless temptations, and that they have in very truth been made "more than conquerors" through Him who loves them.

CHAPTER 11

Difficulties Concerning Failures

The very title of this chapter may perhaps startle some. "Failures. . . ," they will say. "We thought there were no failures in this life of faith!"

There ought not to be and need not be; but, as a fact, there sometimes are, and we must deal with the facts and not with theories. No safe teacher of this interior life ever says that it becomes impossible to sin; they only insist that sin ceases to be a necessity, and that a possibility of continual victory is opened before us. And there are very few, if any, who do not confess that, as to their own actual experience, they have at times been overcome by at least a momentary temptation.

In speaking of sin here, I mean conscious, known sin, not sins of ignorance or what is called the inevitable sin of our nature, which are all met by the provisions of Christ and do not disturb our fellowship with God. A little baby girl was playing about the library one warm summer afternoon, while her father was resting on the lounge. A pretty inkstand on the table took the child's fancy, and unnoticed by anyone, she climbed on a chair and secured it. Then, walking over to her father with an air of childish triumph, she turned it upside down on the white expanse of his shirt bosom and laughed with glee as she saw the black streams trickling down on every side.

This was a very wrong thing for the child to do, but it could not be called sin, for she knew no better. When a believer enters upon the highway of holiness, he finds himself surprised into sin. He is tempted either to be utterly discouraged and to give everything up as lost, or else in order to preserve the doctrines untouched, he feels it necessary to cover up his sin, calling it an infirmity and refusing to be candid and aboveboard about it. Either of these courses is equally fatal to any real growth and progress in the life of holiness. The only way is to face the sad fact at once, call the thing by its right name, and discover, if possible, the reason and the remedy. This life of union with God requires the utmost honesty with Him and with ourselves.

A sudden failure is no reason for being discouraged and giving up all as lost. Neither is the integrity of our doctrine touched by it. We are not preaching a *state*, but a *walk*. The highway of holiness is not a *place*, but a *way*. Sanctification is not a thing to be picked up at a certain stage of our experience and forever after possessed, but it is a life to be lived day by day and hour by hour. We may for a moment turn aside from a path, but the path is not obliterated by our wandering and can be instantly regained. The great point is an instant return to God. Our sin is no reason for ceasing to trust but only an unanswerable argument why we must trust more fully than ever. From whatever cause we have been betrayed into failure, it is very certain that there is no remedy to be found in discouragement. A child who is learning to walk may lie down in despair when he has fallen and refuse to take another step; a believer who is seeking to learn how to live and walk by faith may give up in despair because of having fallen into sin. The only way in both cases is to get right up and try again. When the children of Israel had met with that disastrous defeat, soon after their entrance into the land, before the little city of Ai, they were all so utterly discouraged that we read: "Wherefore the hearts of the people melted, and became as water. And Joshua rent his clothes, and fell to the earth upon his face before the ark of the LORD until the eventide, he and the elders of Israel, and put dust upon their heads. And Joshua said, Alas, O, Lord GOD, wherefore hast thou at all brought this people over Jordan, to deliver us into the hand of the Amorites, to destroy us? would to God we had been content, and dwelt on the other side Jordan! O LORD, what shall I say, when Israel turneth their backs before their enemies!"

What a wail of despair this was! And how exactly it is repeated by many a child of God in the present day, whose heart, because of a defeat, melts and becomes as water. He cries out, "Would to God we had been content, and dwelt on the other side Jordan!" and predicts for itself further failures and even utter discomfiture before its enemies. No doubt Joshua thought then, as we are apt to think now, that discouragement and despair were the only proper and safe condition after such a failure. But God thought otherwise. "And the LORD said unto Joshua, Get thee up; wherefore liest thou thus upon thy face?"

A little girl once expressed this feeling to me with a child's outspoken candor. She asked whether the Lord Jesus always forgave us for our sins as soon as we asked Him, and I had said, "Yes, of course He does."

"*Just* as soon?" she repeated doubtingly.

"Yes," I replied, "the very minute we ask, He forgives us."

"Well," she said deliberately, "I cannot believe that. I should think He would make us feel sorry for two or three days first. And then I should think He would make us ask Him a great many times and in a very pretty way, too, not just in common talk. And I believe that *is* the way He does, and you need not try to make me think He forgives me right at once, no matter what the Bible says."

She only *said* what most Christians *think*, and what is worse, what most Christians act on, making their discouragement and their very remorse separate them infinitely further off from God than their sin would have done. Yet it is so totally contrary to the way we like our children to act toward us that I wonder how we ever could have conceived such an idea of God. How a mother grieves when a naughty child goes off alone in despairing remorse and doubts her willingness to forgive; and how, on the other hand, her whole heart goes out in welcoming love to the repentant little one who runs to her at once and begs her forgiveness! The fact is that the same moment that brings the consciousness of sin ought to bring also the confession and the consciousness of forgiveness. We can only walk this path by "looking continually unto Jesus," moment by moment. And if our eyes are turned away from Him to look upon our own sin and our own weakness, we shall leave the path at once. The believer who has entered upon this highway must flee with it instantly to the Lord, if he finds himself overcome by sin. But he must do as the children of Israel did, rise up "*early* in the morning," and "*run*" to the place where the evil thing is hidden and take it out of its hiding place, and lay it "out before the LORD." He must confess his sin. And then he must stone it with stones and burn it with fire and utterly put it away from him and raise over it a great heap of stones that it may be forever hidden from his sight. He must claim by faith an immediate forgiveness and an immediate cleansing and must go on trusting harder and more absolutely than ever.

As soon as Israel's sin had been brought to light and put away, God's word came again in a message of glorious encouragement: "Fear not, neither be thou dismayed. . .see, I have given into thy hand the king of Ai, and his people, and his city, and his land." Our courage must rise higher than ever, and we must abandon ourselves more completely to the Lord that His mighty power may the more perfectly work in us "all the good pleasure of His will." We must forget our sin as soon as it is thus confessed and forgiven. We must not dwell on it and examine it and indulge in a luxury of distress and remorse. An earnest Christian man, an active worker in the church, had been living for several months in an experience of great peace and joy. He was suddenly overcome by a temptation to treat a brother unkindly. He spent three years of utter misery going further and further away from God and being gradually drawn off into one sin after another until his life was a curse to himself and to all around him. His health failed under the terrible burden, and his reason threatened to fail him. Later a Christian lady who understood this truth about sin that I have been trying to explain found out his trouble in a few minutes' conversation. At once he said, "You sinned in that act. There is no doubt about it, and I do not want you to try to excuse it. But have you never confessed it to the Lord and asked Him to forgive you?"

"Confessed it!" he exclaimed. "Why, it seems to me I have done nothing but confess it and beg God to forgive me, night and day, for all these three dreadful years."

"And you have never believed He did forgive you?" asked the lady.

"No," said the poor man, "how could I, for I never *felt* as if He did."

"But suppose He had said He forgave you— would not that have done as well as for you to feel it?"

"Oh yes," replied the man. "If God said it, of course I would believe it."

"Very well, He does say so," was the lady's answer. She turned to the verse we have taken above (1 John 1:9) and read it aloud. "Now," she continued, "you have been all these three years confessing and confessing your sin, and all the while God's record has been declaring that He was faithful and just to forgive it and to cleanse you, and yet you have never once believed it. You have been 'making God a liar' all this while by refusing to believe His record."

The poor man saw the whole thing and was

dumb with amazement and consternation. When the lady proposed that they should kneel down and he should confess his past unbelief and sin and should claim, then and there, a present forgiveness and a present cleansing, he obeyed like one in a maze. But the result was glorious. The light broke in, his darkness vanished, and he began aloud to praise God for the wonderful deliverance. In a few minutes his soul was enabled to traverse back by faith the whole long weary journey that he had been three years in making, and he found himself once more resting in the Lord and rejoicing in the fullness of His salvation.

The truth is, the only remedy, after all, is to trust in the Lord. And if this is all we ought to do and all we can do, is it not better to do it at once? It is a life and walk of *faith* we have entered upon; and if we fail in it, our only recovery must lie in an increase of faith, not in a lessening of it.

Let every failure then, if any occur, drive you instantly to the Lord with a more complete abandonment and a more perfect trust. If you do this, you will find that, sad as it is, your failure has not taken you out of the land of rest nor broken for long your sweet communion with Him.

Having shown the way of deliverance from failure, I would now say a little as to the causes of failure in this life of full salvation. The causes do not lie in the strength of the temptation, nor in our own weakness, nor above all in any lack in the power or willingness of our Savior to save us. The promise to Israel was positive: "There shall not any man be able to stand before thee all the days of thy life." And the promise to us is equally positive: "God is faithful, who will not suffer you to be tempted above that ye are able; but will with the temptation also make a way to escape, that ye may be able to bear it." Anything cherished in the heart which is contrary to the will of God, let it seem ever so insignificant or be ever so deeply hidden, will cause us to fall before our enemies. The moment, therefore, that a believer who is walking in this interior life meets with a defeat, he must at once seek for the cause, not in the strength of that particular enemy, but in something behind—some hidden want of consecration lying at the very center of his being. I believe our blessed guide, the indwelling Holy Spirit, is always secretly discovering these things to us by continual little checks and pangs of conscience so that we are left without excuse. But it is very easy to disregard His gentle voice and insist upon it to ourselves that all is right while the fatal evil continues hidden in our midst, causing defeat in most unexpected quarters.

We had moved into a new house, and in looking over it to see if it was all ready for occupancy, I noticed in the cellar a very clean-looking cider cask headed up at both ends. I debated with myself whether I should have it taken out of the cellar and opened to see what was in it but decided to leave it undisturbed. I did not feel quite easy but reasoned away my scruples and left it. Every spring and fall, when housecleaning time came on, I would remember that cask with a little twinge of my housewifely conscience, feeling I could not quite rest in the thought of a perfectly clean house while it remained unopened. For two or three years the innocent-looking cask stood quietly in our cellar. Then, most unaccountably, moths began to fill our house. I used every possible precaution against them and made every effort to eradicate them but in vain. They increased rapidly and threatened to ruin everything we had. I suspected our carpets as being the cause and subjected them to a thorough cleaning. I suspected our furniture and had it newly upholstered. I suspected all sorts of impossible things. At last the thought of the cask flashed on me. At once I had it brought up out of the cellar and the head knocked in, and I think it safe to say that thousands of moths poured out. In the same way, some innocent-looking habit or indulgence, some apparently unimportant and safe thing, about which, however, we have now and then little twinges of conscience—something which is not brought out fairly into the light and investigated under the searching eye of God—lies at the root of most of the failure in this interior life. *All* is not given up. Some secret corner is kept locked against the entrance of the Lord. Some evil thing is hidden in the recesses of our hearts, and therefore we cannot stand before our enemies but find ourselves smitten down in their presence.

In order to prevent failure or to discover its cause if we find we have failed, it is necessary to keep continually before us this prayer: "Search me, O God, and know my heart; try me, and know my thoughts: and see if there be any wicked way in me, and lead me in the way everlasting."

Let me beg of you, however, dear Christians, do not think because I have said all this about failure that I believe in it. There is no necessity for it whatever. The Lord Jesus *is* able, according to the declaration concerning Him, to deliver us out of the hands of our enemies that we may "serve him without fear, in holiness and righteousness before him, all the days of our life."

CHAPTER 12

Is God in Everything?

One of the greatest obstacles to an unwavering experience in the interior life is the difficulty of seeing God in everything. People say, "I can easily submit to things that come from God, but I cannot submit to man, and most of my trials and crosses come through human instrumentality." Or they say, "It is all well enough to talk of trusting, but when I commit a matter to God, man is sure to come in and disarrange it all. And while I have no difficulty in trusting God, I do see serious difficulties in the way of trusting men."

Nearly everything in life comes to us through human instrumentalities, and most of our trials are the result of somebody's failure or ignorance or carelessness or sin. We know God cannot be the author of these things, and yet, unless He is the agent in the matter, how can we say to Him about it, "Thy will be done"?

Moreover, things in which we can see God's hand always have a sweetness in them that comforts while it wounds. But the trials inflicted by man are full of nothing but bitterness.

What is needed, then, is to see God in everything and to receive everything directly from His hands with no intervention of second causes. And it is to this that we must be brought before we can know an abiding experience of entire abandonment and perfect trust. Our abandonment must be to God, not to man. And our trust must be in Him, not in any arm of flesh, or we shall fail at the first trial.

The question here confronts us at once, "But is God in everything, and have we any warrant from the scripture for receiving everything from His hands without regarding the second causes that may have been instrumental in bringing them about?" I answer to this, unhesitatingly, "Yes." To the children of God, everything comes directly from their Father's hand, no matter who or what may have been the apparent agents. There are no "second causes" for them.

The whole teaching of scripture asserts and implies this. Not a sparrow falls to the ground without our Father. The very hairs of our head are all numbered. We are not to be careful about anything, because our Father cares for us. We are not to avenge ourselves, because our Father has charged Himself with our defense. We are not to fear, for the Lord is on our side. No one can be against us, because He is for us. We shall not want, for He is our Shepherd. When we pass through the rivers, they shall not overflow us, and when we walk through the fire, we shall not be burned, because He will be with us. He shuts the mouths of lions that they cannot hurt us. "He hath said, 'I will never leave thee, nor forsake thee.' So that we may boldly say, The Lord is my helper, and I will not fear what man shall do unto me."

To my own mind, these scriptures, and many others like them, settle forever the question as to the power of "second causes" in the life of the children of God. Second causes must all be under the control of our Father, and not one of them can touch us except with His knowledge and by His permission. It may be the sin of man that originates the action, and therefore the thing itself cannot be said to be the will of God; but by the time it reaches us, it has become God's will for us and must be accepted as directly from His hands. No man or company of men, no power in earth or heaven can touch that soul that is abiding in Christ without first passing through His encircling presence and receiving the seal of His permission. If God be for us, it matters not who may be against us; nothing can disturb or harm us except He shall see that it is best for us and shall stand aside to let it pass.

If the child is in his father's arms, nothing can touch him without the father's consent unless he is too weak to prevent it. And even if this should be the case, he suffers the harm first in his own person before he allows it to reach his child. How much more will our heavenly Father, whose love is infinitely greater and whose strength and wisdom can never be baffled, care for us! I am afraid there are some, even of God's own children, who scarcely think that He is equal to themselves in tenderness and love and thoughtful care, and who, in their secret thoughts, charge Him with a neglect and indifference of which they would feel themselves incapable. The truth really is that His care is infinitely superior to any possibilities of human care and that He, who counts the very hairs of our heads and suffers not a sparrow to fall without Him, takes note of the minutest matters that can affect the lives of His children and regulates them all according to His own perfect will, let their origin be what they may.

The instances of this are numberless. Take Joseph. What could have seemed more apparently on the face of it the result of sin and utterly contrary to the will of God than the action of his brothers in selling him into slavery? And yet Joseph, in speaking of it, said, "As for you, ye thought evil against me; but God meant it unto good." It was undoubtedly sin in Joseph's brothers, but by the time it had reached Joseph, it had become God's will for him and was, in truth, though he did not see it then, the greatest blessing of his whole life. I learned this lesson practically and through experience long years before I knew the scriptural truth concerning it. I was attending a prayer meeting held in the interests of the life of faith when a strange lady rose to speak. I looked at her, wondering who she could be, little thinking she was to bring a message to my soul that would teach me a grand practical lesson. She said she had great difficulty in living the life of faith on account of the second causes that seemed to her to control nearly everything that concerned her. Her perplexity became so great that at last she began to ask God to teach her the truth about it, whether He really was in everything or not. After praying this for a few days, she had what she described as a vision. She thought she was in a perfectly dark place, and there advanced toward her, from a distance, a body of light that gradually surrounded and enveloped her and everything around her. As it approached, a voice seemed to say, "This is the presence of God! This is the presence of God!" While surrounded with this presence, all the great and awful things in life seemed to pass before her—fighting armies, wicked men, raging beasts, storms and pestilences, sin and suffering of every kind. She shrank back at first in terror. But she soon saw that the presence of God so surrounded and enveloped herself and each one of these things, that not a lion could reach out its paw, nor a bullet fly through the air, except as the presence of God moved out of the way to permit it. And she saw that if there were ever so thin a film, as it were, of this glorious presence between herself and the most terrible violence, not a hair of her head could be ruffled, nor anything touch her, except as the presence divided to let the evil through. Then all the small and annoying things of life passed before her; and equally she saw that there also she was so enveloped in this presence of God that not a cross look, nor harsh word, nor petty trial of any kind could affect her, unless God's encircling presence moved out of the way to let it.

Her difficulty vanished. Her question was answered forever. God *was* in everything. Would that it were only possible to make every Christian see this truth as plainly as I see it! For I am convinced it is the only clue to a completely restful life.

I once heard of a poor woman who earned a precarious living by daily labor but was a joyous, triumphant Christian.

"Ah, Nancy," said a gloomy Christian lady to her one day, who almost disapproved of her constant cheerfulness and yet envied it. "Ah, Nancy, it is all well enough to be happy now, but I should think the thoughts of your future would sober you. Only suppose, for instance, that you should have a spell of sickness and be unable to work. Or suppose your present employers should move away and no one else should give you anything to do; or suppose—"

"Stop!" cried Nancy. "I never supposes. De Lord is my shepherd, and I knows I shall not want. And, honey," she added to her gloomy friend, "it's all dem *supposes* as is makin' you so mis'able. You'd better give dem all up and just trust de Lord."

Nothing else but this: Seeing God in everything will make us loving and patient with those who annoy and trouble us.

Nothing else will completely put an end to all murmuring or rebelling thoughts. If our Father permits a trial to come, it must be because the trial is the sweetest and best thing that could happen to us, and we must accept it with thanks from His dear hand. This does not mean, however, that we must like or enjoy the trial itself, but that we must like God's will in the trial. A good illustration of this may be found in the familiar fact of a mother giving medicine to her dearly loved child. The bottle *holds* the medicine, but the mother *gives* it; so the bottle is not responsible, but the mother.

The human beings around us are often the bottles that hold our medicine, but it is our Father's hand of love that pours out the medicine and compels us to drink it.

Shall we rebel against the human bottles then? Shall we not rather take thankfully from our

Father's hand the medicine they contain?

If He always has His way, then we always have our way also, and we reign in a perpetual kingdom. He who sides with God cannot fail to win in every encounter; and whether the result is joy or sorrow, failure or success, death or life, we may under all circumstances join in the apostle's shout of victory, "Thanks be unto God, which always causeth us to triumph in Christ!"

PART III

Results

CHAPTER 13

Bondage or Liberty

There are two kinds of Christian experience, one of which is an experience of bondage and the other an experience of liberty.

In the first case, the soul is controlled by a stern sense of duty and obeys the laws of God, either from fear of punishment or from expectation of wages. In the other case, the controlling power is an inward life principle that works out, by the force of its own motions or instincts, the will of the divine Life Giver without fear of punishment or hope of reward. In the first, the Christian is a servant and works for hire; in the second, he is a son and works for love.

There ought not to be this contrast in the experience of Christians, for to "walk at liberty" is plainly their only right and normal condition. But as we have to deal with what is, rather than with what ought to be, we cannot shut our eyes to the sad condition of bondage in which so many of God's children pass a large part of their Christian lives. The reason is legality, and the remedy is Christ.

In the epistle to the Galatians, some Jewish brothers had come among the churches in Galatia and, by representing that certain forms and ceremonies were necessary to their salvation, had tried to draw them away from the liberty of the gospel. And with these teachers Peter had allowed himself to unite. Therefore Paul reproves, not only the Galatians, but also Peter himself.

Neither Peter nor the Galatians had committed any moral sin, but they had committed a spiritual sin. They had gotten into a wrong attitude of soul toward God—a legalistic attitude. They began in the right attitude. But when it came to a question of how they were to live in this life, they had changed their ground. They had sought to substitute works for faith. We are, however, continually tempted to forget that it is not what men *do* that is the vital matter, but rather what they *are*. God is a great deal more concerned about our really *being* "new creatures" than about anything else, because He knows that if we *are* right as to our inward being, we shall certainly *do* right as to our outward actions.

Paul was grieved with the Galatian Christians because they seemed to have lost sight of this vital truth—that the inward life, the "new creature," was the only thing that availed. This passage is the only one in which the expression "fallen from grace" is used in the New Testament, and it means that the Galatians had made the mistake of thinking that something else besides Christ was necessary for their right Christian living. The Jewish brothers who had come among them had taught them that Christ alone was not enough, but that obedience to the ceremonial law must be added.

They added the ceremonial law; *we* add resolutions, or agonizings, or Christian work, or churchgoing, or religious ceremonies of one sort or another. It does not make much difference what you add; the wrong thing is to add anything at all.

The following contrasts may help some to understand the difference between these two kinds of religion and may also enable them to discover where the secret of their own experience of legal bondage lies:

The law says, This do, *and you shall live.*

The gospel says, Live, *and then you shall do.*

The law says, Pay *me what you owe.*

The gospel says, I frankly forgive *you all.*

The law says, Make *you a new heart and a new spirit.*

The gospel says, A new heart will I give you, and a new spirit will I put within you.

The law says, Thou shalt love the LORD *thy God with all thine heart, and with all thy soul, and with all thy might.*

The gospel says, Herein is love, not that we loved God, but that he loved us, and sent his Son to be the propitiation for our sins.

The law says, Cursed *is every one who continues not in all things written in the book of the law to do them.*
The gospel says, Blessed *is the man whose iniquities are forgiven, and whose sins are covered.*

The law says, The wages *of sin is death.*
The gospel says, The gift *of God is eternal life through Jesus Christ our Lord.*

The law demands *holiness.*
The gospel gives *holiness.*

The law says, Do.
The gospel says, Done.

The law extorts *the unwilling service of a bondman.*

The gospel wins *the loving service of a son and
    freeman.*
The law makes blessings the result of obedience.
The gospel makes obedience the result of
    blessings.

*The law places the day of rest at the end of the
    week's work.*
The gospel places it at its beginning.

The law says, If.
The gospel says, Therefore.

*The law was given for the restraint of the old
    man.*
*The gospel was given to bring liberty to the new
    man.*

Under the law, salvation was wages.
Under the gospel, salvation is a gift.

Paul tells us that the law "is our schoolmaster,"
not our savior, bringing us to Christ. After faith
in Christ is come, he declares, we are no longer
to be under a schoolmaster. He uses the contrast
between a servant and a son as an illustration of his
meaning. "Wherefore," he says, "thou art no more
a servant, but a son." It is as if a woman had been
a servant in a house, paid for her work in weekly
wages, and under the law of her master, whom she

had tried to please, but toward whom her service had been one of duty only. Finally, however, the master offers her his love and lifts her up from the place of a servant to be his bride and to share his fortunes. At once the whole spirit of her service is changed. She may perhaps continue to do the same things that she did before, but she does them now altogether from a different motive. The old sense of duty is lost in the new sense of love. The cold word *master* is transformed into the loving word *husband*. Imagine this bride feeling unworthy of union with her husband and to lose consequently the inward sense of this union. Who can doubt that very soon the old sense of working for wages would drive out the new sense of working for love? What happens to many Christians now? The servitude of duty takes the place of the service of love; and God is looked upon as the stern taskmaster who demands our obedience instead of as the loving Father who wins it.

Nothing so destroys the sweetness of any relation as the creeping in of this legalistic spirit. The moment a husband and wife cease to perform their services to each other out of a heart of love and union and begin to perform them from a sense of duty alone, that moment the sweetness of the union is lost, and the marriage tie becomes a bondage, and things that were a joy before are turned into crosses. Legalistic Christians do not deny Christ, they only seek to add something to Christ. Their idea is, Christ—and something besides. But to add anything to Christ, no matter how good it may be, as the procuring cause of salvation, is to deny His completeness and to exalt self. People will undergo many painful self-sacrifices rather than take the place of utter helplessness and worthlessness. A man will gladly be a Saint Simeon Stylites or even a fakir if only it is self that does it so that self may share the glory. And a religion of bondage always exalts self. It is what *I* do—*my* efforts, *my* wrestlings, *my* faithfulness. But a religion of liberty leaves self nothing to glory in. It is all Christ, and what He does, and what He is, and how wonderfully He saves.

I once had a friend whose Christian life was a life of bondage. She worked for her salvation harder than any slave ever worked to purchase his freedom. "What would you think," I asked, "of children who had to wrestle and agonize with their parents every morning for their necessary food and clothing, or of sheep that had to wrestle with their shepherd before they could secure the necessary care?"

"Of course I see that would be all wrong," she said, "but then why do I have such good times after I have gone through these conflicts?"

This puzzled me for a moment, but then I asked, "What brings about those good times finally?"

"Why, finally," she replied, "I come to the point of trusting the Lord."

"Suppose you should come to that point to begin with?" I asked.

"Oh," she replied, with a sudden illumination, "I never until this minute thought that I might!"

Christ says that except we "become as little children" we cannot enter into the kingdom of heaven. But it is impossible to get the child spirit until the servant spirit has disappeared. Notice, I do not say the spirit of service, but the servant spirit. Every good child is filled with the spirit of service but ought not to have anything of the servant spirit. The child serves from love; the servant works for wages.

One servant of whom we read in the Bible thought his lord was a "hard master," and the spirit of bondage makes us think the same now. Whenever any of the children of God find themselves "walking at liberty," they at once begin to think there must be something wrong in their experience because they no longer find anything to be a "cross" to them. Sometimes I think that the whole secret of the Christian life that I have been trying to describe is revealed in the child relationship. Nothing more is needed than just to believe that God is as good a Father as the best ideal earthly father. Children do not need to carry about in their own pockets the money for their support. It is not necessary for Christians to have all their spiritual possessions in their own keeping.

It is far better that their riches should be stored up for them in Christ, and that when they want anything they should receive it directly from His hands.

Sometimes a great mystery is made out of the life hidden with Christ in God. This contrast between bondage and liberty makes it very plain. It is only to find out that we really are "no more servants, but sons," and practically to enter into the blessed privileges of this relationship. All can understand what it is to be a little child; there is no mystery about that. They are their Father's heirs and may enter now into possession of all that is necessary for their present needs.

It is because legalistic Christians do not know the truth of their relationship to God, as children to a father, and do not recognize His fatherly heart toward them, that they are in bondage. When they do recognize it, the spirit of bondage becomes impossible to them.

Our liberty must come, therefore, from an understanding of the mind and thoughts of God toward us.

"Against such there is no law," is the divine sentence concerning all who live and walk in the Spirit; and you shall find it most blessedly true in your own experience if you will but lay aside all self-effort and self-dependence of every kind and will consent to let Christ live in you and work in you and be your indwelling life.

The man who lives by the power of an inward righteous nature fulfills the law in his soul and is therefore free. The other rebels against the law in his soul and is therefore bound.

Abandon yourselves so utterly to the Lord Jesus Christ that He may be able to "work in you all the good pleasure of His will," and may, by the law of the Spirit of life in Himself, deliver you from every other law that could possibly enslave you.

CHAPTER 14

Growth

One great objection made against those who advocate this life of faith is that they do not teach a growth in grace. They are supposed to teach that the soul arrives in one moment at a state of perfection, beyond which there is no advance, and that all the exhortations in the scriptures that point toward growth and development are rendered void by this teaching.

Since exactly the opposite of this is true, I will try, if possible, to answer these objections and to show what seems to me the scriptural way of growing and in what place the soul must be in order to grow.

The text that is most frequently quoted is 2 Peter 3:18: "But grow in grace, and in the knowledge of our Lord and Savior Jesus Christ."

Now, this text expresses exactly what we who teach this life of faith believe to be God's will for us, and what we also believe He has made it possible for us to experience. We believe in a growing that does really produce continually progressing maturity and in a development that, as a fact, does bring forth ripe fruit. We expect to reach the aim set before us. No parent would be satisfied with the growth of his child if day after day and year after year he remained the same helpless babe he was in the first months of his life. And no farmer would feel comfortable under such growing of his grain as should stop short at the blade and never produce the ear or the full corn in the ear. Growth, to be real, must be progressive, "Ah! But, Mrs. Smith, I believe in *growing* in grace." "How long have *you* been growing?" I asked. "About twenty-five years," was her answer. "And how much more unworldly and devoted to the Lord are you now than when your Christian life began?" I continued. "Alas!" was the answer. "I fear I am not nearly so much so." The trouble with her, and with every other such case, is simply this: They are trying to grow *into* grace, instead of *in* it. They are like a rosebush, planted by a gardener in the hard, stony path, with a view to its growing *into* the flower bed and which has of course dwindled and withered in consequence instead of flourishing and maturing. When the children of Israel started on their wanderings at Kadesh Barnea, they were at the borders of the land, and a few steps would have taken them into it. When they ended their wanderings in the plains of Moab, they were also at its borders, only with this difference: that now there was a river to cross, which at first there would not have been. To get possession of this land, it was necessary first to be in it; and to grow in grace, it is necessary first to be planted in grace. When once in the land, however, their conquest was rapid; and when once planted in grace, the growth of the spiritual life becomes vigorous and rapid beyond all conceiving. For grace is a most fruitful soil, and the plants that grow therein are plants of a marvelous growth. They are tended by the divine Husbandman and are warmed by the Sun of Righteousness and watered by the dew from heaven. Surely it is no wonder that they bring forth fruit, "some an hundredfold, some sixtyfold, some thirtyfold."

Grace is the unhindered, wondrous, boundless love of God, poured out upon us in an infinite variety of ways, without stint or measure, not according to our deserving but according to His measureless heart of love. Put together all the tenderest love you know of—the deepest you have ever felt and the strongest that has ever been poured out upon you—and heap upon it all the love of all the loving human hearts in the world, and then multiply it by infinity, and you will begin perhaps to have some faint glimpses of the love and grace of God!

To "grow in grace," therefore, the soul must be planted in the very heart of this divine love, enveloped by it, steeped in it. It must let itself out to the joy of it and must refuse to know anything else. It must grow in the apprehensions of it, day by day; it must entrust everything to its care and must have no shadow of doubt but that it will surely order all things well.

To grow in grace is to put our growing, as well as everything else, into the hands of the Lord and leave it with Him. It is to grow as the lilies grow, or as the babies grow, without care and without anxiety; to grow because He who has planted us has planted a growing thing and has made us on purpose to grow.

Surely this is what our Lord meant when He said, "Consider the lilies of the field, how they grow; they toil not, neither do they spin: and yet I say unto you, that even Solomon in all his glory was not arrayed like one of these." Or, when He says again, "Which of you by taking thought can add one cubit unto his stature?" There is no effort in the growing of a babe or of a lily. The lily does not toil or spin; it does not stretch or strain; it does not make any effort of any kind to grow; it is not conscious even that it is growing. The result of this sort of growing in the Christian life is sure. Even Solomon in all his glory, our Lord says, was not arrayed like one of God's lilies. Solomon's array cost much toiling and spinning, and gold and silver in abundance, but the lily's array costs none of these. And though we may toil and spin to make for ourselves beautiful spiritual garments and may strain and stretch in our efforts after spiritual growth, we shall accomplish nothing. For no man by taking thought *can* add one cubit to his stature, and no array of ours can ever equal the beautiful dress with which the great Husbandman clothes the plants that grow in His garden of grace and under His fostering care.

What we all need is to "consider the flowers of the field" and learn their secret. Grow, grow in God's way, which is the only effectual way. See to it that you are planted in grace, and then let the divine Husbandman cultivate you in His own way and by His own means. Put yourselves out in the sunshine of His presence and let the dew of heaven come down upon you and see what will be the result. Leaves and flowers and fruit must surely come in their season; for your Husbandman is skillful, and He never fails in His harvesting. Only see to it that you oppose no hindrance to the shining of the Sun of Righteousness or the falling of the dew from heaven. The thinnest covering may serve to keep off the sunshine and the dew, and the plant may wither, even where these are most abundant. And so also the slightest barrier between your soul and Christ may cause you to dwindle and fade as a plant in a cellar or under a bushel. Bask in the sunshine of His love.

Drink of the waters of His goodness. Keep your face upturned to Him as the flowers do to the sun. Look, and your soul shall live and grow.

We are not inanimate flowers but intelligent human beings with personal powers and personal responsibilities. What the flower is by nature, we must be by an intelligent and free surrender. To be one of God's lilies means an interior abandonment of the rarest kind. It means that we are to be infinitely passive and yet infinitely active also; passive as regards self and its workings, active as regards attention and response to God. Self must step aside to let God work.

You need make no efforts to grow, therefore; but let your efforts instead be all concentrated on this, that you abide in the Vine. The divine Husbandman who has the care of the Vine will care also for you who are His branches and will so prune and purge and water and tend you that you will grow and bring forth fruit. Put yourselves absolutely into the hands of the good Husbandman, and He will at once begin to make the very desert blossom as the rose and will cause springs and fountains of water to start up out of its sandy wastes. Our divine Husbandman is able to turn any soil, whatever it may be like, into the soil of grace the moment we put our growing into His hands. He does not need to transplant us into a different field; but right where we are, with just the circumstances that surround us, He makes His sun to shine and His dew to fall upon us and transforms the very things that were before our greatest hindrances into the chief and most blessed means of growth.

Let yourselves grow. No difficulties in your case can baffle Him. If you will only put yourselves absolutely into His hands and let Him have His own way with you, no dwarfing of your growth in the years that are past, no apparent dryness of your inward springs of life, no crookedness or deformity in your development can in the least mar the perfect work that He will accomplish. "Consider the lilies of the field, *how they grow*; they toil not, neither do they spin." These words give us the picture of a life and growth far different from the ordinary life and growth of Christians—a life of rest and a growth without effort; and yet a life and a growth crowned with glorious results. We may rest assured that all the resources of God's infinite grace will be brought to bear on the growing of the tiniest flower in His spiritual garden as certainly as they are in His earthly creation. As the violet abides peacefully in its little place, content to receive its daily portion without concerning itself about the wandering of the winds or the falling of the rain, so must we repose in the present moment as it comes to us from God. This is the kind of "growth in grace" in which we who have entered into the life of full trust believe; a growth without care or anxiety on our part, but a growth that does actually grow. We rejoice to know that there are many such plants growing up now in the Lord's heritage. They are like the lilies. As the lilies behold the face of the sun and grow thereby, they are, by "beholding as in a glass the glory of the Lord," being changed into the same image from glory to glory, even as by the Spirit of the Lord.

They grow so rapidly and with such success, their answer would be that they are not concerned about their growing and are hardly conscious that they do grow. Their Lord has told them to abide in Him and has promised that, if they do thus abide, they shall certainly bring forth much fruit. They are content to leave the cultivating and the growing and the training and the pruning to their good Husbandman. Let us look at the subject practically. We all know that growing is not a thing of effort but is the result of an inward life principle of growth. All the stretching and pulling in the world could not make a dead oak grow, but a live oak grows without stretching. It is plain, therefore, that the essential thing is to get within you the growing life, and then you cannot help but grow. And this life is the "life hid with Christ in God," the wonderful divine life of an indwelling Holy Spirit. Be filled with this, dear believer, and whether you are conscious of it or not, you cannot help growing. Say a continual yes to your Father's will. And finally, in this, as in all the other cares of your life, "Be careful for nothing; but in every thing by prayer and supplication with thanksgiving, let your requests be made known unto God. And the peace of God, which passeth all understanding, shall keep your hearts and minds through Christ Jesus."

CHAPTER 15

Service

There is, perhaps, no part of Christian experience where a greater change is known upon entering into this life hid with Christ in God than in the matter of service.

In all the ordinary forms of Christian life, service is apt to have more or less of bondage in it. That is, it is done purely as a matter of duty and often as a trial and a cross. Certain things, which at the first may have been a joy and a delight, become after a while weary tasks, performed faithfully, perhaps, but with much secret disinclination and many confessed or unconfessed wishes that they need not be done at all, or at least that they need not be done so often. The soul finds itself asking, instead of the "May I?" of love, the "Must I?" of duty. The yoke, which was at first easy, begins to gall, and the burden feels heavy instead of light.

One dear Christian expressed it once to me in this way: "When I was first converted," she said, "I was so full of joy and love that I was only too glad and thankful to be allowed to do anything for my Lord, and I eagerly entered every open door. But after a while, as my early joy faded away, and my love burned less fervently, I began to wish I had not been quite so eager; for I found myself involved in lines of service that were gradually becoming very distasteful and burdensome to me. Since I had begun them, I could not very well give them up without provoking much talk, and yet I longed to do so increasingly. I was expected to visit the sick and pray beside their beds. I was expected to attend prayer meetings and speak at them. I was expected, in short, to be always ready for every effort in Christian work, and the sense of these expectations bowed me down continually. At last it became so unspeakably burdensome to me to live the sort of Christian life I had entered upon, and was expected by all around me to live, that I felt as if any kind of manual labor would have been easier. And I would have infinitely preferred scrubbing all day on my hands and knees to being compelled to go through the treadmill of my daily Christian work." Does this give a vivid picture of some of your own experiences, dear Christian? Have you never gone to your work as a slave to his daily task, believing it to be your duty and that therefore you must do it, but rebounding like an India rubber ball back into your real interests and pleasures the moment your work was over?

Or, if this does not describe your case, perhaps another picture will. You do love your work in the abstract, but in the doing of it you find so many cares and responsibilities connected with it and feel so many misgivings and doubts as to your own capacity or fitness that it becomes a very heavy burden, and you go to it bowed down and weary before the labor has even begun. Then also you are continually distressing yourself about the results of your work. Now, from all these forms of bondage the soul that enters fully into the blessed life of faith is entirely delivered. Service of any sort becomes delightful to it because, having surrendered its will into the keeping of the Lord, He works in it to will and to do of His good pleasure, and the soul finds itself really *wanting* to do the things God wants it to do. It is always very pleasant to do the things we *want* to do, let them be ever so difficult of accomplishment or involve ever so much of bodily weariness. If a man's *will* is really set on a thing, he regards with a sublime indifference the obstacles that lie in the way of his reaching it and laughs to himself at the idea of any opposition or difficulties hindering him. Many men have scorned the thought of any "cross" connected with it! It is all in the way we look at things. What we need in the Christian life is to get believers to *want* to do God's will as much as other people want to do their own will. It is what God intended for us, what He has promised. In describing the new covenant in Hebrews 8:6–13, He says, "I will put my laws into their mind, and write them in their hearts." This can mean nothing but that we shall *love* His law, for anything written in our hearts we must love. "And putting it into our mind" is surely the same as God working in us to "will and to do of his good pleasure," and means that we shall will what God wills and shall obey His sweet commands, not because it is our duty to do so, but because we ourselves want to do what He wants us to do.

And we, who are by nature a stiff-necked people, always rebel more or less against a law from outside of us while we joyfully embrace the same law springing up within.

God's way of working, therefore, is to get possession of the inside of a man, to take the control and management of his will, and to work it for him. If you are in bondage in the matter of service, you need to put your will over completely into the hands of your Lord, surrendering to Him the entire control of it. In one case, a lady had been for years rebelling fearfully against a little act of service that she knew was right but which she hated. I saw her, out of the depths of despair, and without any feeling whatever, give her will in that matter up into the hands of her Lord and begin to say to Him, "Thy will be done; *Thy will be done!*" And in one short hour, that very thing began to look sweet and precious to her.

It is wonderful what miracles God works in wills that are utterly surrendered to Him. Also there is deliverance in the wonderful life of faith. For in this life no burdens are carried, no anxieties felt. The Lord is our burden-bearer, and upon Him we must lay off every care. He says, in effect, "Be careful for nothing, but make your requests known to Me, and I will attend to them all." Be careful for *nothing*, He says, not even your service. Above all, I should think, our service, because we know ourselves to be so utterly helpless in regard to it, that, even if we were careful, it would not amount to anything. What have we to do with thinking whether we are fit or not? The Master Workman surely has a right to use any tool He pleases for His own work, and it is plainly not the business of the tool to decide whether it is the right one to be used or not. He knows, and if He chooses to use us, of course we must be fit. And in truth, if we only knew it, our chief fitness is in our utter helplessness. His strength is made perfect, not in our strength, but in our weakness. Our strength is only a hindrance.

It is no wonder that Paul could say, "Most gladly

therefore will I rather *glory* in my infirmities, that the power of Christ may rest upon me." If the work is His, the responsibility is His also, and we have no room left for worrying about results. The most effectual workers I know are those who do not feel the least care or anxiety about their work, but who commit it all to their dear Master, and, asking Him to guide them moment by moment in reference to it, trust Him implicitly for each moment's needed supplies of wisdom and of strength.

There are one or two other bonds in service from which this life of trust delivers us. We find out that no one individual is responsible for all the work in the world, but only for a small share. Our duty ceases to be universal and becomes personal and individual. The Master does not say to us, "Go and do everything," but He marks out a special path for each of us and gives to each one of us a special duty. There are "diversities of gifts" in the kingdom of God, and these gifts are divided to "every man according to his several ability." I may have five talents or two or only one. I may be called to do twenty things or only one. My responsibility is simply to do that which I am called to do and nothing more. "The *steps* of a good man are ordered of the LORD," not his way only, but each separate step in that way.

Once a young Christian who, because she had been sent to speak a message to one soul whom she met while on a walk, supposed it was a perpetual obligation and thought she must speak to everyone she met on her walks about their souls. This was of course impossible, and as a consequence she was soon in hopeless bondage about it. She became absolutely afraid to go outside of her own door and lived in perpetual condemnation. At last this friend told her just to put herself under the Lord's personal guidance as to her work and trust Him to point out to her each particular person to whom He would have her speak, assuring her that He never puts forth His own sheep without going before them and making a way for them Himself. She followed this advice and laid the burden of her work on the Lord, and the result was a happy pathway of daily guidance in which she was led into much blessed work for her Master and was able to do it all without a care or a burden because He led her out and prepared the way before her.

Years ago I came across this sentence in an old book: "Never indulge, at the close of an action, in any self-reflective acts of any kind, whether of self-congratulation or of self-despair. Forget the things that are behind the moment they are past, leaving them with God." When the temptation comes, as it mostly does to every worker after the performance of any service, to indulge in these reflections, either of one sort or the other, I turn from them at once and positively refuse to think about my work at all, leaving it with the Lord to overrule the mistakes and to bless it as He chooses. To sum it all up, then, what is needed for happy and effectual service is simply to put your work into the Lord's hands and leave it there. Even in the midst of a life of ceaseless activity, you shall "find rest to your soul."

Be also yielded unto Him as "instruments of righteousness," to be used by Him as He pleases!

CHAPTER 16

Practical Results in the Daily Walk and Conversation

If all that has been written in the foregoing chapters on the life hid with Christ be true, its results in the practical daily walk and conversation ought to be very marked, and the people who have entered into the enjoyment of it ought to be, in very truth, a peculiar people, zealous of good works.

My son, now with God, once wrote to a friend something to this effect: that we are God's witnesses necessarily, because the world will not read the Bible, but they will read our lives; and that upon the report these give will very much depend their belief in the divine nature of the religion we possess. If, therefore, our faith is to make any headway in the present time, it must be proved to be more than a theory; and we must present to the investigation of the critical minds of our age the realities of lives transformed by the mighty power of God, "working in them all the good pleasure of His will."

I desire, therefore, to speak very solemnly for what I conceive to be the necessary fruit of a life of faith such as I have been describing and to press home to the hearts of every one of my readers their personal responsibility to "walk worthy of the high calling" with which they have been called.

The standard of practical holy living has been so low among Christians that the least degree of real devotedness of life and walk is looked upon with surprise and often even with disapproval by a large portion of the Church. And for the most part, the followers of the Lord Jesus Christ are satisfied with a life so conformed to the world and so like it in almost every respect that to a casual observer, no difference is discernible.

We who have heard the call of our God to a life of entire consecration and perfect trust must do differently. We must come out from the world and be separate. We must set our affections on heavenly things, not on earthly ones, and we must seek first the kingdom of God and His righteousness, surrendering everything that would interfere with this. We must walk through the world as Christ walked. We must have the mind that was in Him. As pilgrims and strangers, we must abstain from fleshly lusts that war against the soul. As good soldiers of Jesus Christ, we must disentangle ourselves inwardly from the affairs of this life that we may please Him who has chosen us to be soldiers. We must abstain from all appearance of evil. We must be kind to one another, tenderhearted, forgiving one another, even as God, for Christ's sake, has forgiven us. We must not resent injuries or unkindness but must return good for evil and turn the other cheek to the hand that smites us. We must take always the lowest place among our fellowmen and seek not our own honor, but the honor of others. We must be gentle and meek and yielding, not standing up for our own rights, but for the rights of others. We must do everything, not for our own glory, but for the glory of God. And, to sum it all up, since He who has called us is holy, so we must be holy in all manner of conversation.

Some Christians seem to think that all the requirements of a holy life are met when there is very active and successful Christian work. Because they do so much for the Lord in public, they feel a liberty to be cross and ugly and un-Christlike in private. We must be just as Christlike to our servants as we are to our minister. In daily home life, indeed, that practical piety can best show itself, and we may well question any "professions" that fail under this test of daily life.

A cross Christian or an anxious Christian, a

discouraged, gloomy Christian, a doubting Christian, a complaining Christian, an exacting Christian, a selfish Christian, a cruel, hard-hearted Christian, a self-indulgent Christian, a Christian with a sharp tongue or bitter spirit—all these may be very earnest in their work and may have honorable places in the church, but they are *not* Christlike Christians. The life hid with Christ in God is a hidden life, as to its source, but it must not be hidden as to its practical results. We must prove that we "possess" that which we "profess." We must really and absolutely turn our backs on everything that is contrary to the perfect will of God. It means that we are to be a "peculiar people," not only in the eyes of God, but in the eyes of the world around us; and that wherever we go, it will be known from our habits, our tempers, our conversation, and our pursuits that we are followers of the Lord Jesus Christ and are not of the world, even as He was not of the world. We must no longer look upon our money as our own, but as belonging to the Lord, to be used in His service. We must not feel at liberty to use our energies exclusively in the pursuit of worldly means but must recognize that, if we seek first the kingdom of God and His righteousness, all needful things shall be added unto us. Our days will have to be spent, not in serving ourselves, but in serving the Lord, and we shall find ourselves called upon to bear one another's burdens and so fulfill the law of Christ. Whatever we do will be done "not with eyeservice, as menpleasers, but as the servants of Christ, doing the will of God from the heart."

Into all this we shall undoubtedly be led by the Spirit of God if we give ourselves up to His guidance. I have noticed that wherever there has been a faithful following of the Lord in a consecrated soul, several things have, sooner or later, inevitably followed.

Meekness and quietness of spirit become in time the characteristics of the daily life. A submissive acceptance of the will of God, as it comes in the hourly events of each day, is shown; pliability in the hands of God to do or to suffer all the good pleasure of His will; sweetness under provocation; calmness in the midst of turmoil and bustle; a yielding to the wishes of others, and an insensibility to slights and affronts; absence of worry or anxiety; deliverance from care and fear. God's glory, and the welfare of His creatures, become the absorbing delight of the soul. Year after year such Christians are seen to grow more unworldly, more serene, more heavenly minded, more transformed, more like Christ until even their very faces express so much of the beautiful inward divine life that all who look at them cannot but take knowledge of them that they live with Jesus and are abiding in Him.

Have you not begun to feel dimly conscious of the voice of God speaking to you, in the depths of your soul, about these things? Has it not been a pain and a distress to you of late to discover how full your lives are of self? Has not your soul been plunged into inward trouble and doubt about certain dispositions or pursuits in which you have been formerly accustomed to indulge? Have you not begun to feel uneasy with some of your habits of life and to wish that you could do differently in certain respects? Have not paths of devotedness and of service begun to open out before you with the longing thought, *Oh, that I could walk them!* All these questions and doubts and this inward yearning are the voice of the Good Shepherd in your heart, seeking to call you out of that which is contrary to His will. Let me entreat of you not to turn away from His gentle pleadings! The heights of Christian perfection can only be reached by each moment faithfully following the Guide who is to lead you there. He reveals the way to us one step at a time, in the little things of our daily lives, asking only on our part that we yield ourselves up to His guidance. Obey Him perfectly the moment you are sure of His will.

I knew a soul thus given up to follow the Lord wherever He might lead her, who in a very little while traveled from the depths of darkness and despair into the realization and actual experience of a most blessed union with the Lord Jesus Christ. Out of the midst of her darkness, she consecrated herself to the Lord, surrendering her will up altogether to Him that He might work in her to will and to do of

His own good pleasure. Immediately He began to speak to her by His Spirit in her heart, suggesting to her some little acts of service for Him and troubling her about certain things in her habits and her life, showing her where she was selfish and un-Christlike and how she could be transformed. She recognized His voice and yielded to Him each thing He asked for the moment she was sure of His will. Her swift obedience was rewarded by a rapid progress, and day by day she was conformed more and more to the image of Christ until very soon her life became such a testimony to those around her that some even who had begun by opposing and disbelieving were forced to acknowledge that it was of God and were won to a similar surrender. If you would know a like blessing, abandon yourself, like her, to the guidance of your divine Master and shrink from no surrender for which He may call.

Things small to you may be in His eyes the key and the clue to the deepest springs of your being. No life can be complete that fails in its little things. A look, a word, a tone of voice even, however small they may seem to human judgment, are often of vital importance in the eyes of God. Whether you knew it or not, this, and nothing less than this, is what your consecration meant. It meant inevitable obedience. It meant that the will of your God was henceforth to be your will. You surrendered your liberty of choice. It meant an hourly following of Him, wherever He might lead you, without any turning back.

Let everything else go that you may live out, in a practical daily walk and conversation, the Christ-life you have dwelling within you. Day by day you will find Him bringing you more and more into conformity with His will in all things, molding you and fashioning you, as you are able to bear it, into a "vessel unto His honor, sanctified and meet for His use, and fitted to every good work." So shall be given to you the sweet joy of being an "epistle of Christ, known and read of all men"; and your light shall shine so brightly that men seeing not you but your good works shall glorify not you but your Father which is in heaven.

CHAPTER 17

The Joy of Obedience

Having spoken of some of the difficulties in this life of faith, let me now speak of some of its joys. And foremost among these stands the joy of obedience.

Long ago I came across this sentence somewhere: "Perfect obedience would be perfect happiness, if only we had perfect confidence in the power we were obeying." The rest has been revealed to me, not as a vision but as a reality. I have seen in the Lord Jesus the Master to whom we may yield up our implicit obedience and, taking His yoke upon us, may find our perfect rest.

You little know, dear hesitating soul, of the joy you are missing. The Master has revealed Himself to you and is calling for your complete surrender, and you shrink and hesitate. A measure of surrender you are willing to make and think indeed it is fit and proper that you should. But a *total* abandonment, without any reserves, seems to you too much to be asked for. You are afraid of it. It involves too much, you think, and is too great a risk. To be measurably obedient you desire; to be perfectly obedient appalls you.

You see other souls who seem able to walk with easy consciences in a far wider path than that which appears to be marked out for you. It seems strange, and perhaps hard to you, that you must do what they need not and must leave undone what they have liberty to do.

Your Lord says, "He that *hath* my commandments, and keepeth them, he it is that loveth me: and he that loveth me shall be loved of my father, and I will love him, and will manifest myself to him." You *have* His commandments; those you envy have them not. *You* know the mind of your Lord about many things, in which, as yet, *they* are walking in darkness. Is it a cause for regret that your soul is brought into such near and intimate relations with your Master that He is able to tell you things that those who are farther off may not know? Do you not realize what a tender degree of intimacy is implied in this?

Many relations in life require from the different parties only very moderate degrees of devotion. We may have really pleasant friendships with one another and yet spend a large part of our lives in separate interests and widely differing pursuits. When together, we may greatly enjoy one another's society and find many congenial points, but separation is not any especial distress to us, and other and more intimate friendships do not interfere. There is not enough love between us to give us either the right or the desire to enter into and share one another's most private affairs. Other relationships in life are different. The friendship becomes love. The two hearts give themselves to a union of the soul. Separate interests and separate paths in life are no longer possible. The deepest desire of each heart is that it may know every secret wish or longing of the other in order that it may fly on the wings of the wind to gratify it.

Do they not rather glory in these very obligations and inwardly pity, with a tender yet exulting joy, the poor far-off ones who dare not come so near? If you have ever loved any of your fellow human beings enough to find sacrifice and service on their behalf a joy; if a wholehearted abandonment of your will to the will of another has ever gleamed across you as a blessed and longed-for privilege or as a sweet and precious reality, then, by all the tender, longing love of your heavenly lover, I would entreat you to let it be so toward Christ!

He loves you with more than the love of friendship. As a bridegroom rejoices over his bride, so does He rejoice over you, and nothing but the bride's surrender will satisfy Him. He has given you all, and He asks for all in return. The slightest reserve will grieve him to the heart. He spared not Himself, and how can you spare yourself? For your sake He poured out in a lavish abandonment all that He had, and for His sake you must pour out all that you have, without stint or measure.

If, then, you are hearing the loving voices of your Lord calling you out into a place of nearness to Himself that will require a separation from all else and that will make an enthusiasm of devotedness not only possible, but necessary, will you shrink or hesitate? Will you think it hard that He reveals to you more of His mind than He does to others, and that He will not allow you to be happy in anything that separates you from Himself? Do you *want* to go where He cannot go with you or to have pursuits that He cannot share?

No! You will spring out to meet His lovely will with an eager joy. You will glory in the very narrowness of the path He marks out for you. The perfect happiness of perfect obedience will dawn upon your soul, and you will begin to know something of what Jesus meant when He said, "I *delight* to do thy will, O my God."

Do you think the joy in this will be all on your side? My friends, we are not able to understand this—the delight, the satisfaction, the joy our Lord has in us. That *we* should need Him is easy to comprehend; that *He* should need us seems incomprehensible. Continually at every heart He is knocking, asking to be taken in as the supreme object of love. "Will you have Me," He says to the believer, "to be your beloved? Will you follow Me into suffering and loneliness and endure hardness for My sake and ask for no reward but My smile of approval and My word of praise? Will you throw yourself, with a passion of abandonment, into My will? Will you give up to Me the absolute control of yourself and of all that you have? Will you be content with pleasing Me, and Me only? May I have My way with you in all things? Will you come into so close a union with Me as to make a separation from the world necessary? Will you accept Me for your heavenly Bridegroom, and leave all others to cleave only to Me?"

In a thousand ways He makes this offer of union with Himself to every believer. But all do not say yes to Him. Other loves and other interests seem to them too precious to be cast aside. They do not miss the joy of heaven because of this. But they miss an unspeakable present joy.

You, however, are not one of these. From the very first your soul has cried out eagerly and gladly to all His offers, "Yes, Lord, yes!" The life of love upon which you have entered gives you the right to a lavish outpouring of *all* of you upon your beloved One. An intimacy and friendship, which more distant souls cannot enter upon, become now, not only your privilege, but also your duty. Your Lord can make known His secrets, and to you He looks for an instant response to every requirement of His love.

What a wonderful, glorious, unspeakable privilege upon which you have entered! How little it will matter to you if men shall hate you and shall separate you from their company and shall reproach you and cast out your name as evil for His dear sake! You may well "rejoice in that day, and leap for joy," for behold, your reward is great in heaven; for if you are a partaker of His suffering, you shall also be of His glory.

He sees in you the "travail of His soul" and is satisfied. Your love and devotedness are His precious reward for all He has done for you. It is unspeakably sweet to Him. Do not be afraid, then, to let yourself go in a heart-whole devotedness to your Lord that can brook *no* reserves. Others may not approve, but He will, and that is enough. Do not stint or measure your obedience or your service. Let your heart and your hand be as free to serve Him as His heart and hand were to serve you. Let Him have all there is of you—body, soul, mind, spirit, time, talents, voice, everything. Lay your whole life open before Him that He may control it. Do not let there be a day nor an hour in which you are not consciously doing His will and following Him wholly.

Christ Himself, when He was on earth, declared the truth that there was no blessedness equal to the blessedness of obedience. It is more blessed to hear and obey His will than to have been the earthly mother of our Lord or to have carried Him in our arms and nourished Him at our breasts!

May our surrendered hearts reach out with an eager delight to discover and embrace the lovely will of our loving God!

CHAPTER 18

Divine Union

All the dealings of God with the soul of the believer are in order to bring them into oneness with Himself. "That they all may be one; as thou, Father, art in me, and I in thee, that they also may be one in us."

This divine union was the glorious purpose in the heart of God for His people before the foundation of the world. It was accomplished in the death of Christ. God has not hidden it or made it hard, but the eyes of many are too dim, and their hearts too unbelieving for them to grasp it. It is therefore for the purpose of bringing His people into the personal and actual realization of this that the Lord calls upon them so earnestly and so repeatedly to abandon themselves to Him.

The usual course of Christian experience is pictured in the history of the disciples. First they were awakened to see their condition and their need, and they came to Christ and gave their allegiance to Him. Then they followed Him, worked for Him, believed in Him; and yet how unlike Him they were! Seeking to be set up one above the other running away from the cross, misunderstanding His mission and His words, forsaking their Lord in time of danger, they were still sent out to preach, recognized by Him as His disciples, and they possessed power to work for Him. They knew Christ only "after the flesh," as outside of them, their Lord and Master, but not yet their life.

Then came Pentecost, and these same disciples came to know Him as He revealed Himself inwardly. From then on He was to them Christ within, working in them to will and to do of His good pleasure, delivering them, by the law of the Spirit of His life, from the bondage to the law of sin and death under which they had been held. No longer was it, between themselves and Him, a war of wills and a clashing of interests. One will alone animated them, and that was His will. One interest alone was dear to them, and that was His. They were made *one* with Him.

Perhaps as yet the final stage of it has not been fully reached. You may have left much to follow

Christ. You may have believed on Him, worked for Him, and loved Him, yet may not be like Him. Allegiance you know and confidence you know, but not yet union. There are two wills, two interests, two lives. You have not yet lost your own life that you may live only in His. Once it was "I and not Christ." Next it was "I and Christ." Perhaps now it is even "Christ and I." But has it come yet to be Christ only and not I at all?

All you need, therefore, is to understand what the scriptures teach about this marvelous union, that you may be sure it is really intended for you.

If you read such passages as 1 Corinthians 3:16, "Know ye not that ye are the temple of God, and that the Spirit of God dwelleth in you?" and then look at the opening of the chapter, you will see that this soul-union of which I speak, this unspeakably glorious mystery of an indwelling of God, is the possession of even the weakest and most failing believer in Christ. Every believer in the "body is the temple of the Holy Ghost."

But although this is true, it is also equally true that unless the believer knows it and lives in the power of it, it is to him as though it were not. This union with Christ is not a matter of emotions, but of character. It is not something we are to *feel*, but something we are to *be*. We may feel it very blessedly, and probably shall, but the vital thing is not the feeling, but the reality.

No one can be one with Christ who is not

Christlike. This is entirely contrary to the scripture declaration that "he that *saith* he abideth in him ought himself also so to *walk*, even as He walked." There is no escape from this, for it is not only a divine declaration but is in the very nature of things as well.

Oneness with Christ means being made a "partaker of his nature," as well as of His life; for nature and life are, of course, one.

If we are really one with Christ, therefore, it will not be contrary to our nature to be Christlike and to walk as He walked, but it will be in accordance with our nature. Sweetness, gentleness, meekness, patience, long-suffering, charity, and kindness will all be natural to the Christian who is a partaker of the nature of Christ. It could not be otherwise.

But people who live in their emotions do not always see this. They *feel* so at one with Christ that they look no further than this feeling, and they often delude themselves with thinking they have come into the divine union, when all the while their nature and dispositions are still under the sway of self-love.

We all know that our emotions are most untrustworthy and are largely the result of our physical condition or our natural temperaments. It is a fatal mistake, therefore, to make them the test of our oneness with Christ. This mistake works both ways. If I have very joyous emotions, I may be deluded by thinking I have entered into the divine union when I have not; and if I have no emotions, I may grieve over my failure to enter when I really have entered.

Character is the only real test. God is holy, and those who are one with Him will be holy also. Our Lord Himself expressed His oneness with the Father in such words as these: "The Son can do nothing of himself, but what he seeth the Father do: for what things soever he doeth, these also doeth the Son likewise." The test Christ gave, then, by which the reality of His oneness with the Father was known, was the fact that He did the works of the Father. And I know no other test for us now.

It is forever true in the nature of things that a tree is known by its fruit. If we have entered into the divine union, we shall bear the divine fruit of a Christlike life and conversation. Pay no regard to your feelings, therefore, in this matter of oneness with Christ, but see to it that you have the really vital fruits of a oneness in character and walk and mind. Undeveloped Christians often have very powerful emotional experiences. I knew one who was kept awake often by the "waves of salvation," but who yet did not tell the truth in her interaction with others and was very far from honest in her business dealings. No one could possibly believe that she knew anything about a real divine union, in spite of all her fervent emotions in regard to it.

Your joy in the Lord is a far deeper thing

than a mere emotion. It is the joy of knowledge, of perception, of actual existence. It is as though Christ were living in a house, shut up in a far-off closet, unknown and unnoticed by the dwellers in the house, longing to make Himself known to them and to be one with them in all their daily lives and share in all their interests, but unwilling to force Himself upon their notice, because nothing but a voluntary companionship could meet or satisfy the needs of His love. The days pass by over that favored household, and they remain in ignorance of their marvelous privilege. They come and go about all their daily affairs with no thought of their wonderful guest. Their plans are laid without reference to Him. His wisdom to guide and His strength to protect are all lost to them. Lonely days and weeks are spent in sadness, which might have been full of the sweetness of His presence.

Suddenly the announcement is made, "The Lord is in the house!" How will its owner receive the intelligence? Will he call out an eager thanksgiving and throw wide open every door for the entrance of his glorious guest? Or will he shrink and hesitate, afraid of His presence, and seek to reserve some private corner for a refuge from his all-seeing eye?

It is far more glorious to be brought into such a real and actual union with Him as to be one with Him—one will, one purpose, one interest, one life—than it would be to have Christ a dweller in the house or in the heart. And yet it ought to be expressed, and our souls ought to be made so unutterably hungry to realize it that day or night we shall not be able to rest without it. It seems too wonderful to be true that such poor, weak, foolish beings as we are should be created for such an end as this; and yet it is a blessed reality. We are even *commanded* to enter into it. We are exhorted to lay down our own lives that His life may be lived in us; we are asked to have no interests but His interests, to share His riches, to enter into His joys, to partake of His sorrows, to manifest His likeness, to have the same mind as He had, to think and feel and act and walk as He did.

Shall we consent to all this? The Lord will not force it on us, for He wants us as His companions and His friends, and a forced union would be incompatible with this. It must be voluntary on our part. The bride must say a willing yes to the bridegroom, or the joy of their union is wanting. It is a very simple transaction and yet very real. The steps are but three: first, be convinced that the scriptures teach this glorious indwelling of God; then surrender our whole selves to Him to be possessed by Him; and finally, we must believe that He *has* taken possession and *is* dwelling in us. We must begin to reckon ourselves dead and to reckon Christ as our only life. It will help us to say, "I am crucified with Christ: nevertheless I live, yet not I, but Christ liveth in me," over and over, day and night, until it becomes the habitual breathing of our souls. We must put off our self-life by faith continually and put on the life of Christ; and we must do this, not only by faith, but practically as well. We must continually put self to death in all the details of daily life and must let Christ instead live and work in us. I mean, we must never do the selfish thing, but always the Christlike thing. We must let this become, by its constant repetition, the attitude of our whole being. As surely as we do, we shall come at last to understand something of what it means to be made one with Christ as He and the Father are one. Christ left all to be joined to us; shall we not also leave all to be joined to Him?

CHAPTER 19

The Chariots of God

It has been well said that "earthly cares are a heavenly discipline," but they are even something better than discipline—they are God's chariots, sent to take the soul to its high places of triumph.

They do not look like chariots. They look instead like enemies, sufferings, trials, defeats, misunderstandings, disappointments, unkindnesses. Could we see them as they really are, we should recognize them as chariots of triumph in which we may ride to those very heights of victory for which our souls have been longing and praying. The chariot of God is the invisible.

The king of Syria came up against the man of God with horses and chariots that could be seen by every eye, but God had chariots that could be seen by none save the eye of faith. The servant of the prophet could only see the outward and visible; and he cried, as so many have done since, "Alas, my master! how shall we do?" but the prophet himself sat calmly within his house without fear, because his eyes were opened to see the invisible; and all he asked for his servant was, "LORD, I pray thee open his eyes, that he may see."

This is the prayer we need to pray for ourselves and for one another, for the world all around us, as well as around the prophet, is full of God's horses and chariots, waiting to carry us to places of glorious victory. And when our eyes are thus opened, we shall see in all the events of life, whether great or small, whether joyful or sad, a "chariot" for our souls.

Everything that comes to us becomes a chariot the moment we treat it as such. If we climb up into them, as into a car of victory, and make them carry us triumphantly onward and upward, they become the chariots of God.

Whenever we mount into God's chariots, the same thing happens to us spiritually that happened to Elijah. We shall have a translation. We shall be carried away from the low, earthly, groveling plane of life, where everything hurts and everything is unhappy, up into the "heavenly places in Christ Jesus," where we can ride in triumph over all below.

These are interior, and the road that leads to them is interior. But the chariot is generally some outward loss or trial or disappointment that afterward "yieldeth the peaceable fruit of righteousness."

In the Song of Solomon we are told of "chariots paved with love." We cannot always see the love-lining to our own particular chariot. It often looks very unlovely. It may be a cross-grained relative or friend; it may be the result of human malice or cruelty or neglect; but every chariot sent by God must necessarily be paved with love since God is love, and God's love is the sweetest, softest, tenderest thing to rest one's self upon that was ever found by any soul anywhere. It is His love, indeed, that sends the chariot.

Look upon your chastenings then, no matter how grievous they may be for the present, as God's chariots sent to carry your souls into the "high places" of spiritual achievement and uplifting, and you will find that they are, after all, "paved with love."

The Bible tells us that when God went forth for the salvation of His people, then He "did ride upon His horses and chariots of salvation"; and it is the same now. The clouds and storms that darken our skies and seem to shut out the shining of the Sun of Righteousness are really only God's chariots. Have you made the clouds in your life your chariots? Are you "riding prosperously" with God on top of them all?

I knew a lady who had a very slow servant. She

was an excellent girl in every other respect and very valuable in the household, but her slowness was a constant source of irritation to her mistress, who was naturally quick, and who always chafed at slowness. This lady would consequently get out of temper with the girl twenty times a day, and twenty times a day she would repent of her anger and resolve to conquer it, but in vain. Her life was made miserable by the conflict. One day it occurred to her that she had for a long while been praying for patience, and that perhaps this slow servant was the very chariot the Lord had sent to carry her soul over into patience. She immediately accepted it as such and from that time used the slowness of her servant as a chariot for her soul. The result was a victory of patience that no slowness of anybody was ever after able to disturb.

I knew another lady, at a crowded convention, who was put to sleep in a room with two others on account of the crowd. *She* wanted to sleep, but *they* wanted to talk; and the first night she was greatly disturbed and lay there fretting and fuming long after the others had hushed, and she might have slept. But the next day she heard something about God's chariots, and at night she accepted these talking friends as her chariots to carry her over into sweetness and patience and was kept in undisturbed calm. When, however, it grew very late, and she knew they all ought to be sleeping, she ventured to say slyly, "Friends, I am lying here riding in a chariot!" The effect was instantaneous, and perfect quiet reigned! Her chariot had carried her over to victory, not only inwardly, but at last outwardly as well.

If we would ride in God's chariots instead of our own, we should find this to be the case continually.

Our constant temptation is to trust in the "chariots of Egypt" or, in other words, in earthly resources. We can *see* them; they are tangible and real and look substantial; while God's chariots are invisible and intangible, and it is hard to believe they are there.

We try to reach high spiritual places with the "multitude of our chariots." We depend first on one thing and then on another to advance our spiritual condition and to gain our spiritual victories. We "go down to Egypt for help." And God is obliged often to destroy all our own earthly chariots before He can bring us to the point of mounting into His.

We lean too much upon a dear friend to help us onward in the spiritual life, and the Lord is obliged to separate us from that friend. We feel that all our spiritual prosperity depends on our continuance under the ministry of a favorite preacher, and he is mysteriously removed. We look upon our prayer meeting or our Bible class as the chief source of our spiritual strength, and we are kept from attending them. And the "chariot of God" which alone can carry us to the place where we hoped to be taken by the instrumentalities upon which we have been depending is to be found in the very deprivations we have so mourned over. With the fire of His love, God must burn up every chariot of our own that stands in the way of our mounting into His.

We have to be brought to the place where all other refuges fail us before we can say, "He only." We say, "He *and*—something else." As long as visible chariots are at hand, the soul will not mount into the invisible ones.

Let us be thankful, then, for every trial that will help to destroy our earthly chariots and that will compel us to take refuge in the chariot of God that stands ready and waiting beside us in every event and circumstance of life. When we mount into God's chariot, our goings are "established," for no obstacles can hinder His triumphal course. All losses, therefore, are gains that bring us to this. Paul understood this, and he glorified in the losses that brought him such unspeakable rewards. "But what things were gain to me, those I counted loss for Christ. Yea doubtless, and I count all things but loss for the excellency of the knowledge of Christ Jesus my Lord: for whom I have suffered the loss of all things, and do count them but dung, that I may win Christ, and be found in him."

Even the "thorn in the flesh," the messenger of Satan sent to buffet him, became a "chariot of God" to his willing soul and carried him to the heights of triumph, which he could have reached in no other way. To "take pleasure" in one's trials—what is this but to turn them into the grandest chariots?

Joseph had a revelation of his future triumphs and reigning, but the chariots that carried him there looked to the eye of sense like dreadful cars of failure and defeat. Slavery and imprisonment are strange chariots to take one to a kingdom, and yet by no other way could Joseph have reached his exaltation. And our exaltation to the spiritual throne that awaits us is often reached by similar chariots.

The great point, then, is to recognize each thing that comes to us as being really God's chariot for us and accept it as from Him. He does not command or originate the thing, perhaps; but the moment we put it into His hands, it becomes His, and He at once turns it into a chariot for us. He makes all things, even bad things, work together for good to all those who trust Him. All He needs is to have it entirely committed to Him.

When your trial comes, then, put it right into the will of God and climb into that will as a little child climbs into her mother's arms. Get into your chariot, then. Take each thing that is wrong in your lives as God's chariot for you. No matter who the builder of the wrong may be, whether men or devils, by the time it reaches your side, it is God's chariot for you and is meant to carry you to a heavenly place of triumph. No doubt the enemy will try to turn your chariot into a juggernaut car by taunting you with the suggestions that God is not in your trouble, and that there is no help for you in Him. But you must utterly disregard all such suggestions and must overcome them with the assertion of a confident faith. "God *is* my refuge and strength, a very present help in trouble" must be your continual declaration, no matter what the "seemings" may be.

You must not be halfhearted about it. You must climb wholly into your chariot, not with one foot dragging on the ground. There must be no "ifs" or "buts" or "supposings" or "questionings." Accept God's will fully and hide yourself in the arms of His love, which are always underneath to receive you in every circumstance and at every moment. Say, "Thy will be done, Thy will be done," over and over. Shut out every other thought but the one thought of submission to His will and of trust in His love. There can be no trials in which God's will has not a place somewhere. The soul has only to mount into His will as in a chariot, and it will find itself "riding upon the heavens" with God in a way it had never dreamed could be.

The soul that thus rides with God "on the sky" has views and sights of things that the soul that grovels on the earth can never have. One dear Christian said to me at the close of a meeting where I had been speaking about these chariots: "I am a poor woman and have all my life long grieved that I could not drive in a carriage like some of my rich neighbors. But I have been looking over my life while you have been talking, and I find that it is so full of chariots on every side that I am sure I shall never need to walk again."

There is no need for any one of us to walk for lack of chariots. That misunderstanding, that mortification, that unkindness, that disappointment, that loss, that defeat—all these are chariots waiting to carry you to the very heights of victory you have so longed to reach.

Mount into them then, with thankful hearts, and lose sight of all second causes in the shining of His love, who will "carry you in His arms" safely and triumphantly over it all.

CHAPTER 20

The Life on Wings

This life hid with Christ in God has one aspect that has been a great help and inspiration to me, and I think may be also to some other longing and hungry souls. It is what I call the life on wings.

This cry for "wings" is as old as humanity. Our souls were made to "mount up with wings," and they can never be satisfied with anything short of flying. Like the captive-born eagle that feels within it the instinct to flight and chafes and frets at its imprisonment, hardly knowing what it longs for, so do our souls chafe and fret and cry out for freedom. We can never rest on earth, and we long to "fly away" from all that so holds and hampers and imprisons us here.

This restlessness and discontent develop

themselves generally in seeking an outward escape from our circumstances or from our miseries. We do not at first recognize the fact that our only way of escape is to "mount up with wings," and we try to "flee on horses," as the Israelites did, when oppressed by their trials (see Isaiah 30:16).

Our "horses" are the outward things upon which we depend for relief, some change of circumstances or some help from man; and we mount on these and run east or west, or north or south, anywhere to get away from our trouble, thinking in our ignorance that a change of our environment is all that is necessary to give deliverance to our souls. But all such efforts to escape are unavailing as we have each one proved hundreds of times. For the soul is not so made that it can "flee upon horses" but must make its flight always upon wings.

Moreover, these "horses" generally carry us, as they did the Israelites, out of one trouble, only to land us in another. How often have we also run from some "lion" in our pathway only to be met by a "bear," or have hidden ourselves in a place of supposed safety, only to be bitten by a "serpent"! No, it is useless for the soul to hope to escape by running away from its troubles to any earthly refuge, for there is not one that can give it deliverance.

There is a glorious way of escape for every one of us if we will but mount up on wings and fly away from it all to God. It is not a way east or west, or north or south, but it is a way upward.

"They that wait upon the LORD shall renew their strength; they shall mount up with wings as eagles; they shall run, and not be weary; and they shall walk, and not faint."

All creatures that have wings can escape from every snare that is set for them if only they will fly high enough, and the soul that uses its wings can always find a sure "way to escape" from all that can hurt or trouble it.

Their secret is contained in the words, "They that wait upon the LORD." The soul that waits upon the Lord is the soul that is entirely surrendered to Him and that trusts Him perfectly. Therefore we must name our wings the wings of Surrender and of Trust. I mean by this that if we will only surrender ourselves utterly to the Lord and trust Him perfectly, we shall find our souls "mounting up with wings as eagles" to the "heavenly places" in Christ Jesus, where earthly annoyance or sorrows have no power to disturb us.

The wings of the soul carry it up into a spiritual plane of life, into the "life hid with Christ in God," which is a life utterly independent of circumstances, one that no cage can imprison and no shackles bind.

Things look very different according to the standpoint from which we view them. The caterpillar, as it creeps along the ground, must have a widely different "view" of the world around it from that which the same caterpillar will have when its wings are developed, and it soars in the air above the very places where once it crawled. And, similarly, the crawling soul must necessarily see things in a very different aspect from the soul that has "mounted up with wings." I was at one time spending a winter in London, and during three long months we did not once see any genuine sunshine because of the dense clouds of smoke that hung over the city like a pall. But many a time I have seen that above the smoke the sun was shining, and once or twice through a rift I have had a glimpse of a bird, with sunshine on its wings, sailing above the fog in the clear blue of the sunlit sky. Not all the brushes in London could sweep away the fog, but if we could only mount high enough, we should reach a region above it all.

And this is what the soul on wings does. It overcomes the world through faith. To overcome means to "come over," not to be crushed under; and the soul on wings flies over the world and the things of it. These lose their power to hold or bind the spirit that is made in very truth "more than a conqueror."

Birds overcome the lower law of gravitation by the higher law of flight; and the soul on wings overcomes the lower law of sin and misery and bondage by the higher law of spiritual flying. The "law of the spirit of life in Christ Jesus" must necessarily be a higher and more dominant law than the law of sin and death; therefore the soul that has mounted into this upper region of the life in Christ cannot fail to conquer and triumph.

But it may be asked how it is, then, that all Christians do not always triumph. A great many Christians do not "mount up with wings" but live on the same low level with their circumstances. On this plane the soul is powerless; it has no weapons with which to conquer there; and instead of overcoming, or coming over, the trials and sorrows of the earthly life, it is overcome by them and crushed under them.

A friend once illustrated to me the difference between three of her friends in the following way. She said, if they should all three come to a spiritual mountain that had to be crossed, the first one would tunnel through it with hard and wearisome labor; the second would meander around it in an indefinite fashion, hardly knowing where she was going, and yet, because her aim was right, getting around it at last; but the third, she said, would just flap her wings and fly right over. If any of us in the past have tried to tunnel our way through the mountains that have stood across our pathway or have been meandering around them, we must resolve to spread our wings and "mount up" into the clear atmosphere of God's presence, where it will be easy to overcome. The largest wings ever known cannot lift a bird one inch upward unless they are used. We must *use* our wings or they avail us nothing.

It is not worthwhile to cry out, "Oh that I had wings, and then I would flee," for we *have* the wings already, and what is needed is not more wings, but only that we should use those we have. The power to surrender and trust exists in every human soul and only needs to be brought into exercise. With these two wings we *can* "flee" to God at any moment, but in order really to reach Him, we must actively use them. We must not merely want to use them, but we must *do* it definitely and actively. We shall not "mount up" very high if we only surrender and trust in theory or in our especially religious moments. We must do it definitely and practically, about each detail of daily life as it comes to us. We must meet our disappointments, our thwartings, our persecutions, our malicious enemies, our provoking friends, our trials and temptations of every sort, with an active and experimental attitude of surrender and trust. We must spread our wings and "mount up" to the "heavenly places in Christ" above them all, where they will lose their power to harm or distress us. Instead of stirring up strife and bitterness by trying, metaphorically, to knock down and walk over our offending brothers and sisters, we should escape all strife by simply spreading our wings and mounting up to the heavenly region where our eyes would see all things covered with a mantle of Christian love and pity.

The mother eagle teaches her little ones to fly by making their nest so uncomfortable that they are forced to leave it and commit themselves to the unknown world of air outside. So does our God to us. He stirs up our comfortable nests and pushes us over the edge of them, and we are forced to use our wings to save ourselves from fatal falling.

With this end in view, we can surely accept with thankfulness every trial that compels us to use our wings, only so they can grow strong and large and fit for the highest flying. Unused wings gradually wither and shrink and lose their flying power; and if we had nothing in our lives that made flying necessary, we might perhaps at last lose all capacity to fly.

A bird may be imprisoned in a cage, or it may be tethered to the ground with a cord, or it may be loaded with a weight that drags it down, or it may be entrapped in the "snare of the fowler." Hindrances that answer to all these in the spiritual realm may make it impossible for the soul to fly until it has been set free from them by the mighty power of God.

One "snare of the fowler" that entraps many souls is the snare of doubt. The doubts look so plausible and often so humble that Christians walk into their "snare" without dreaming for a moment that it is a snare at all until they find themselves caught and unable to fly; for there is no more possibility of flying for the soul that doubts than there is for the bird caught in the fowler's snare.

The reason of this is evident. One of our wings, namely, the wing of trust, is entirely disabled by the slightest doubt; and just as it requires two wings to lift a bird in the air, so does it require two wings to lift the soul. A great many people do everything but trust. They spread the wing of surrender and use it vigorously and wonder why it is that they do not mount up, never dreaming that it is because all the while the wing of trust is hanging idle by their sides. It is because Christians use one wing only that their efforts to fly are often so irregular and fruitless.

It may be that for some the "snare of the fowler" is some subtle form of sin, some hidden want of consecration. Where this is the case, the wing of trust may seem to be all right, but the wing of surrender hangs idly down; and it is just as hopeless to try to fly with the wing of trust alone as with the wing of surrender alone. Both wings must be used, or no flying is possible.

If we find ourselves imprisoned, then, we may be sure of this, that it is not our earthly environment that constitutes our prison-house, for the soul's wings scorn all paltry bars and walls of earth's making. The only thing that can really imprison the soul is something that hinders its upward flight. The prophet tells us that it is our iniquities that have separated God and ourselves, and it is our sins that have hid His face from us. Therefore, if our soul is imprisoned, it must be because some indulged sin has built a barrier between us and the Lord, and we cannot fly until this sin is given up and put out of the way.

But often, where there is no conscious sin the soul is still unconsciously tethered to something of earth and so struggles in vain to fly. Our souls are often not unmoored from earthly things. We must cut ourselves loose. As well might an eagle try to fly with a hundred-ton weight tied fast to its feet as the soul try to "mount up with wings" while a weight of earthly cares and anxieties is holding it down to earth.

We are commanded to have our hearts filled with songs of rejoicing and to make inward melody to the Lord. But unless we mount up with wings, this is impossible, for the only creature that can sing is the creature that flies. When the prophet declared that though all the world should be desolate, yet he would rejoice in God and joy in the God of his salvation, his soul was surely on wings. Paul knew what it was to use his wings when he found himself to be "sorrowful, yet always rejoicing." On the earthly plane all was dark to both Paul and the prophet, but on the heavenly plane all was brightest sunshine.

Do you think that by flying I mean necessarily any very joyous emotions or feelings of exhilaration? There is a great deal of emotional flying that is not real flying at all. It is such flying as a feather accomplishes that is driven upward by a strong puff of wind but flutters down again as soon as the wind ceases to blow. The flying I mean is a matter of *principle*, not a matter of *emotion*. It may be accompanied by very joyous emotions, but it does not depend on them. It depends only upon the facts of an entire surrender and an absolute trust. Every one who will honestly use these two wings and will faithfully persist in using them, will find that they *have* mounted up with wings as an eagle, no matter how empty of all emotion they may have felt themselves to be before.

For the promise is sure: "They that wait upon the LORD. . .*shall* mount up with wings as eagles." Not "may perhaps mount up," but "*shall*." It is the inevitable result. May we each one prove it for ourselves!

Also Available from Barbour Publishing